POST WITH PURPOSE

A DIGITAL STRATEGY HANDBOOK

POST WITH PURPOSE

A DIGITAL STRATEGY HANDBOOK

JEFFREY S. RUM

》》ignite: action
2018

First Printing: 2018

ISBN 978-1-387-20464-9

ignite: action
5523 Southwick Street
Bethesda, Maryland 20817

Ordering Information:

Special discounts are available on quantity purchases by corporations, associations, educators, and others. For details, contact the publisher at the above listed address.

U.S. trade bookstores and wholesalers:
Please contact ignite: action at (202) 607-0964 or books@igniteaction.co.

For Jess, Eva, Max and Ori:
All the purpose I need.

CONTENTS

AUTHOR BIO

Jeff Rum is the Founder and CEO of ignite: action, a marketing agency based in Bethesda, Maryland. Prior to founding ignite: action, he served as President and Chief Marketing Officer at SPARK Experience, a user experience (UX) research and design agency. Rum is well-known in the industry as an award-winning digital marketing strategist, educator and public speaker with nearly 15 years of experience in digital strategy, branding, and marketing.

Rum served as a digital consultant with The White House, United Nations Foundation, Human Rights Campaign and the Elizabeth Edwards Foundation. During his tenure at SPARK, Rum also led digital campaigns and special projects with AAA, Capital Bank, PepsiCo, and Fossil.

Profiled in SmartCEO Magazine and an online panelist for CMSWire, Rum regularly guest lectures at The George Washington University's School of Business on topics including digital marketing and social media strategy.

Rum received his BA from American University in Communications, Visual Media and Jewish Studies and his MA from Georgetown University in International Studies.

ACKNOWLEDGEMENTS

I would like to thank my editor, copyeditor and researcher, Sierra Bellows. Without her professionalism, thoughtfulness and care, this book would not be possible. A special thanks to Jessica Walton for proofreading, final editing, and book marketing.

Thank you to the numerous contributors to this project, including, but not limited to, Amy Blum, Kelsey Crockett, Emily Goodstein, Ahava Leibtag, Sarah Sicherman, Hager Sharp and Noetic Consultants.

To my extended family, friends, colleagues, clients and partners at ignite: action, thank you for the ongoing trust, support and good humor.

Thank you to my 10th grade English and Journalism teacher, Mrs. Irene Ritaccio (Ruop). You saw something in me that no other teacher did. Because of you, I found a passion for the written word.

Thank you to my mom and dad, Paula and Nathan, and my other mom and dad, Jo-Ann and Dan. Family means everything to me and I'm blessed to have such an incredible support system.

Finally, thank you to Jess, the love of my life, and my children Eva, Max and Ori for supporting me continuously through this effort. I love you to the moon and back.

"We have to do with
the past only as we can
make it useful to the
present and the future."

- Frederick Douglass

FOREWORD
BY EMILY GOODSTEIN

This is not a book about social media. This is not really a book about technology, either.

This is a book about people.

I've spent the entirety of my career working to move people to action, first in a grassroots organizing position for a women's health nonprofit and then on the software side of this whole online strategy scene. After that, I decided to go out on my own. As a digital strategy consultant, I get a front row seat for approaches that flow and produce results… and I get urgent calls from potential clients when a lack of strategy or unrealistic plan hasn't yielded results. It was this consulting work that led me to Jeff Rum; he's become a trusted colleague and friend and I'm honored he's involved me in this book.

Thinking back to my first job in the online organizing space: I was a year of out of college and asked to run a national student organizing program. I was given the log-in information for the organization's Facebook feed and Twitter account and told to "run with it." The assumption was made that because I was young and these tools are pretty easy to use, I could make them work to reach the population the program aimed to engage.

What was never discussed was the strategy, measurement, or even realistic goals to determine success. There was no mention of audience selection or the specific folks we were trying to engage, nor the messages that would resonate well with our target population. I'm sure you're shocked to hear that the words "ladder of online engagement" weren't spoken. And most importantly, there wasn't dialogue about how to use the online outreach work we were doing to complement and amplify the work happening offline. In Yiddish this is called a *shanda,* which means shame.

I was able to put together a *somewhat* successful program, but knowing what I know now about how to make the most of these easy-to-use tools, I cringe thinking about all the folks we didn't reach. Or those we reached and then never actually engaged. I was so focused on numbers and thought very little of what to do with people once I had their email address or their prized Facebook "like."

That was almost 15 years ago and so much has changed in the world of online organizing and digital strategy. Mobile, text to give, responsive design… and, dare I say, Snapchat. The field has gotten more sophisticated. Brands have gotten smart about the power of a comprehensive digital plan and nonprofits are following suit.

I don't do this work to help nonprofit staffers report to board members that over 10,000 people have "liked" the most recent Facebook post or that most recent marketing video went viral (although those things are fun, too). I do this work because I believe in the power of online marketing to affect social change.

Post with Purpose is a guide to help you use online marketing strategy to move people... to action. What happens once someone makes an online donation or signs up for your organization's email newsletter? What then? That's what you'll learn from *Post with Purpose*. And so much more.

INTRODUCTION

IT'S GAME TIME

I'll never forget my first tennis tournament in 7th grade. I woke up early, ate a good breakfast, and blasted Billy Joel's "We Didn't Start the Fire" to get pumped. I was a nervous 13-year-old about to play in his first big sports event.

That morning, my father gave me a piece of advice about strategy that I will never forget: Just get the ball over the net, and let your opponent make the mistakes. I repeated that statement in my head while I stood on the court and waited to return the first serve. It worked. I won the match and went on to the finals.

In retrospect, my father's advice was a gift partly because it gave me a strategy instead of focusing on tactics and techniques. A strategy is greater than just tactics. It brings together larger goals and ambitions – the "why" – with tactics – the "how." And, maybe most importantly, a strategy is flexible and can be fit to changing circumstances.

Overall, I was a pretty good tennis player. And I knew my strengths and weaknesses. I had a strong, if inelegant, backhand, but my serve wasn't as powerful as some of my opponents. Luckily, I was fast and tireless, so my father's strategy worked. Eventually, my opponents would get fatigued and make mistakes.

I was not the best player in terms of form and technique. My tactics were a mixed bag. (It's hard to admit that my backhand looked more like a baseball swing than anything else.) There were other tactics that I used, such as playing more aggressively from the baseline or keeping my serves consistent.

Part of my strategy was to study my opponent, to understand his strengths and weaknesses. In addition, I had to stay focused on the goal: getting the ball over the net. When I employed my tactics within the larger framework of a strategy, I won points, which turned into winning games, and ultimately matches.

These lessons in tennis strategy have influenced how I think about digital strategy. There are many digital marketing tactics an organization can use. As this book is being published, another social app will start getting buzz. Furthermore, each organization is going to have its own strengths and weaknesses when it comes to digital marketing techniques. But to focus too much on tactics is to lose the bigger picture.

An organization that wants to make real gains needs a digital strategy that makes the ideals of an organization its highest priority. That strategy must then flexibly employ tactics to respond to a constantly changing digital landscape.

Let's get the ball over the net, shall we?

Plan versus strategy

It's important to know the difference between a plan and a strategy. These two terms are often used interchangeably yet they are quite different. Let's quickly review the differences:

A plan is a list of steps to accomplish a goal. A plan should include specific information about each task in the list, including what the action is, who will enact it, how, when and where. A plan is necessary to achieve almost any complex goal.

"A strategy is bigger than a plan," writes George Konetes, director of digital media at Infinity Concepts in Export, Pennsylvania. "Strategy tackles the question of 'why?' It has a large scope and looks at the end result as well as the many paths to the desired outcome. A strategy looks at every possible influencing factor, both seen and unforeseen and comes to terms with the whole situation, not just one end result."

Strategy comes before planning. Indeed, strategy shapes the specifics of a plan. Strategy focuses on "why," while a plan focuses on "how."

Why a digital strategy?

"A strategy is the overarching wisdom that coordinates all of the plans in order to effectively reach the goals," writes Konetes.

A strategy requires that you know where you're going. I find that organizations without a digital strategy have no direction. They churn out content, information, and advertising. But they have no compass. In short, they don't have strategic online goals.

"In nonprofit organizations the ultimate strategic goal is fulfillment of a social mission – the creation of public value," writes researchers Seungahn Nah and Gregory D. Saxton in a journal article about nonprofits and social media. "The strategy an organization employs to fulfill this mission has implications for its adoption and use of new media."

Organizations without a strategy often fail to ask the big questions: What are they trying to do as an organization? How can digital marketing support those goals? Why are they doing what they do? "Why" questions are hard. They require wrestling with big challenges, understanding the competition, and knowing the target audience really well.

The biggest cost of not having a strategy is that your competitors will leave you in the dust. If you're not dedicating the right resources to digital marketing, or you're flying by the seat of your pants, then your competition will win.

Finally, what is your online value proposition? An online value proposition is a promise of value to be delivered. It leads to a belief, among customers, about how they will benefit from engaging with your organization. Your online value proposition answers the question, "Why should customers interact with you online rather than through another channel? Or with a competitor?" What are you providing your existing and new customers that will make them want to stay loyal? Without a digital strategy, it may be more difficult to keep even those most loyal to your organization.

What does a good value proposition look like for a nonprofit organization? Invisible Children, Inc. is an organization founded in 2004 to increase awareness of the activities of the Lord's Resistance Army in Central Africa, and its leader, Joseph Kony. Its donation page has this text in the second paragraph: "By choosing to donate to Invisible Children today, you are taking an active role in efforts to stop Joseph Kony, protect vulnerable communities, bring abducted soldiers home…" This statement makes the "why" of Invisible Children crystal clear.

What is a digital strategy?

Creating a digital strategy is both a science and an art. There should be form and structure, yet room for creativity. Room for imperfection, for experimentation, and the ability and permission to admit something didn't work. A digital strategy should be nimble and fluid.

But before we look at the fundamentals of digital strategy, let's take a look at the definition.

According to global business strategy consultancies Accenture Strategy and PwC, a digital strategy features the application of new technologies to existing business activity and a focus on the enablement of new digital capabilities to support the business. When formulating a digital strategy, always keep in mind the overall business goal of your organization. A solid digital strategy would include identifying your organization's vision, goals, opportunities, and any other relevant activities in order to maximize the business benefits of the digital initiatives your organization will put into play.

What makes a strategy *digital?* Digital is a descriptor. It means that the set of activities is within the digital space. This is why a digital strategy may be a subset of a larger marketing or business strategy, or it may be a specific need for the organization to focus on a digital solution to a digital challenge.

For example, imagine that your organization's name changes. You need to ensure that the world still knows your name and that business can continue as usual. You create a set of digital campaigns to let everyone know that the organization has a new name. These campaigns use a variety of online channels such as social media and email to reach key audience groups. You track the campaigns using several codes and analytics software. Easy, right?

If only it were that easy.

What a successful campaign looks like

I talked with Hager Sharp, a Washington D.C.-based marketing and communications firm, about campaigns they had run for clients that turned out well. They shared a story about the Lumina Foundation, which is committed to increasing the proportion of Americans who hold postsecondary degrees and certificates in the U.S.

Each year Lumina Foundation publishes a report on the state of the nation's progress toward their goal of having 65 percent of Americans with postsecondary education by 2025. In 2016, Hager Sharp partnered with Lumina to support the release of that report, called the Stronger Nation Report. The work included organizing and promoting an event at the National Press Club, conducting extensive media outreach, and running a strategic social media campaign.

"The goals of our digital and social media efforts were to earn significant engagement, extend the reach of the Stronger Nation release announcement, and generate social conversation about the release prior to, during, and for several weeks after the event," according to Hager Sharp.

How did they do it? Hager Sharp developed a digital strategy that leveraged organic content across Lumina's Facebook, Twitter, and

LinkedIn channels, supplemented by paid promotions on Twitter and LinkedIn. According to Hager Sharp:

> The strategy included secondary research on audiences' digital behavior and media consumption habits, to better understand messages most likely to resonate with each audience— education policymakers, Lumina grantees, and the public— and on what platforms the audiences would be most receptive. We segmented target audience members by geography, focusing on high-priority states for Lumina's policy efforts, age, industry, job function, and other parameters, to ensure reach among those most likely to be interested in the release.

The marketing firm created original content around three themes to help ensure a consistent and compelling narrative around the findings, and then used Google Analytics tracking codes to understand which content themes resonated best on each platform and audience.

And it worked! The Lumina Foundation successfully created nearly two million impressions, more than 15,000 social media engagements, and 6,100 link clicks for the Stronger Nation Report. Paid content generated 81 percent of all its social impressions and 69 percent of all owned social referrals.

Audience for this book

According to Zoe Amar and David Evans, half of charities don't have a digital strategy. Just nine percent have been through the full digital transformation process and embedded it. They write that there are multiple challenges facing organizations "in progressing with digital and maximising results." Fifty-seven percent of those surveyed cite lack of skills as the biggest barrier. "A lack of the right infrastructure but also the wrong culture, and a lack of confidence and agility with digital are also holding charities back. Just under a third want more digital leadership in their charities," write Amar and Evans. "Seventy-five percent of charities think growing their digital skills would help them increase fundraising, whilst 71 percent see opportunities to grow its network and 69 percent to deliver its strategy more effectively."

Let's be honest. A digital strategy is not critical for *every* organization. Some get by just fine without a strategy in place. A small organization may not have the time or the resources to dedicate to creating a digital strategy.

They still may perform digital activities. They tweet. They buy ads online. They send out emails. They do okay. They don't have a critical mass waiting for them to speak out and take a stand on an issue. Their bottom line will not alter too much whether their website is following best practices when it comes to user experience (UX) design or content development. Their digital presence is a small piece of a much larger pie. They rely more heavily on face-to-face relationships. They are not too worried about strategy when it comes to digital marketing and online communication.

Other organizations already have their digital strategy figured out. Their digital strategy is aligned with their business goals and objectives. They have support from the top down and the bottom up. They have developed a sophisticated strategy that is tracked in real-time by multiple teams viewing online dashboards chock full of the right information. This data allows them to make decisions on product offerings, content, and business strategy.

But I would say many organizations are somewhere in the middle. They strive for a more data-driven digital roadmap. They do their best to follow best practices. They send out surveys on occasion to learn from their users. They may hire an outside vendor (or two) to manage some aspects of their digital marketing efforts. They take a closer look at web analytics and try to find ways to measure the work they do. They use social media as a listening device, not just a megaphone. They care about strategy and find ways to optimize conversion, whatever that may be.

This book is for those looking to take all the small pieces – the fragments of digital marketing – and put together a solid strategy that is meaningful, manageable, and measureable. And you'll notice that the framework outlined in this book is geared toward purpose-driven organizations – nonprofits, associations, and NGOs – but it can work for nearly any organization.

In the subsequent pages, you will find a way to make sense of the madness. Digital marketing trends will change monthly, weekly, if not daily. There will be new channels, updated tools, and significant shifts in algorithms. But the fundamentals of building an effective digital strategy are sound. They will not change for some time. They require thinking, planning, designing, and distributing.

Ahava Leibtag, content strategist and president of Aha Media Group, says that when digital strategies fail it is most often because an organization wasn't ready to do the necessary work to make it a success. "Sometimes organizations invest a lot of money and time before they have really thought through what they want to achieve and committed to it. You know how people say that losing weight is a full-time job? You have to commit to it and work at it? It is the same with content strategy," Leibtag says.

Is your organization ready to make the commitment necessary to make a digital strategy work? "The inability to commit to a strategy, like a bad boyfriend, dooms the work to failure," says Leibtag.

Fundamentals of building an effective digital strategy

Thinking. The strategy itself will take some thought. It will be best to have a group work on this, if possible. You don't need marketing experts or digital analysts. It's best to have people who are invested in the organization, people who know your objectives intimately. It may be someone in business strategy, development, or customer service. You'll want to include stakeholders in this process who can champion it from inception to implementation and beyond. You'll want a diversity of ideas, a diversity of skills, and people who care about the organization's future.

Planning. The good news: planning will not take months or years. It can be done in a few meetings, but a digital strategy does require thoughtful planning and a calendar of sorts. This will help keep activities on track and continually connect the day-to-day work to your organization's vision and goals. You will need a spreadsheet or two and perhaps some online software to keep the data in some format that is easily accessible.

Designing. You don't need skills in Photoshop, but you will want to bring out the whiteboard or flipchart to sketch. There are key artifacts that will be outlined in each step of the strategy that will serve as a visual reference for your organization throughout the process. These designs are critical because they bring the strategy to life. They make personas into people. They make goals into stories. They make a spreadsheet become a user (or customer) journey. You can be the world's worst artist, and still be the greatest designer of a digital strategy.

Implementing. What seems like the easiest part often becomes the most challenging. Who will do which activities? How will the strategy be implemented? Who is in charge? How will you hold others accountable? These are questions that all come down to proper delegating of responsibilities—or as I like to call it, a distribution of activities. A core element of a successful digital strategy is making sure that the plan is realistic and expectations are set for every player involved. The team that knows what to do and when to do it will create success. Everyone needs a checklist.

Creating a digital strategy is not rocket science. It takes a certain attitude: one that means business, that can connect the dots, but also one that knows when it's okay to pivot and switch gears. In the digital world especially, strategies need to be robust yet flexible. The framework must be solid, but the design should be fluid and change as necessary. Most importantly, building a digital strategy should be fun. It should be creative.

If the word "strategy" sounds boring or like rigid corporate speak, this book is aimed to contradict that notion. Indeed, a good strategy should bring life, color, purpose, and meaning to an organization, and allow it to better connect with their audience and ignite action in both the digital and real world.

REFERENCES

Amar, Z., & Evans, D. (2016). The Charity Digital Skills Report. Retrieved from http://report.skillsplatform.org/charitydigitalreportdetail/

Konetes, G. (2011, September 19). The Difference Between a Plan and a Strategy. Retrieved from http://infinityconcepts.net/2011/09/the-difference-between-a-plan-and-a-strategy/

Leibtag, A. (2017, May 15). Phone interview

McDonald, M. (2015, March 03). What is a digital strategy? Retrieved from https://www.accenture.com/us-en/blogs/blogs-digital-what-is-digital-strategy

Ricketts, A. (2017, March 23). Report says half of charities do not have digital strategies. Retrieved from https://www.thirdsector.co.uk/report-says-half-charities-not-digital-strategies/digital/article/1428383

Strategy&. (2017). Strategy& is PwC's strategy consulting team. Retrieved from https://www.strategyand.pwc.com/global/home/who_we_are

Zhuang, J., Saxton, G. D., & Wu, H. (2011). Publicity vs. impact in nonprofit disclosures and donor preferences: a sequential game with one nonprofit organization and N donors. *Annals of Operations Research,221*(1), 469-491. doi:10.1007/s10479-011-0967-3

CHAPTER 1
DEFINE YOUR WHY

Why does your organization exist? No, really. *Why* does it exist?
I don't mean what are your business goals or fundraising goals, or
what products do you make, or what services do you provide, or how
much money would you like to make. I mean *why* do you do what you
do? Why is it important, essential, or different? Why does it matter?
What do you believe?

Think about the brands and products you love or the organizations
you support – the ones you are fiercely loyal to. Your loyalty doesn't
grow because you like the color selection of the products, or because
you thought the print ad used a nice font, or they have good shipping
costs. You are loyal to the brands and products you love because you
identify with their ethos. Because they *have* an ethos, a belief system.
Those organizations have a compelling, emotional, and persuasive
answer to the question: *Why do you do what you do?*

Knowing why is the beginning of any good digital strategy

The very first step in an organized digital strategy is defining your "why," but it's a step many organizations ignore or rush past—or don't think about at all. But if you don't nail the answer to this question, everything that comes after it will lack the most basic driving principle you have: the reason why your organization actually matters.

One of my favorite marketing teaching methods is Simon Sinek's landmark TED Talk, "Start With Why." In it, he persuasively lays out the logic behind starting with "why." Most organizations, he says, begin with "what," creating a marketing strategy through explaining what they do. But that's not what compels people. And neither does explaining "how" an organization does what it does, however innovative that process is. While what you do and how you do it are absolutely important components of an organization, they aren't the core reasons why people have those pre-verbal positive responses. The core reason behind those automatic positive responses happens when an organization communicates its unique and emotionally moving reason for *existing*.

"Every organization knows what they do," Sinek says. "Most know how they do it. Almost no one knows why they do it."

And that right there is the number one reason I have organizations begin to shape a digital strategy by answering the question of why they exist. It not only serves as the basis of every marketing effort from there on out, but it sets them apart from the competition in an immediate, emotional way.

Start with what you know: from what to why

Even though our goal is to land at the "why," don't be afraid to start with the "what." In fact, many organizations might find that to be the easiest place to start. After all, every employee knows what the organization does.

Let's look at some examples.

National Gaucher Foundation, a nonprofit that raises awareness and provides resources for those with a rare genetic disease, went through a Sinek-inspired exercise on moving through the Golden Circle to get at the heart of the organization.

"To get to the 'why,' we first discussed 'what' our organization does and 'how,'" says Executive Director Amy Blum. "This was in and of itself enlightening and created an energy in the room."

That energy isn't accidental. It can be eye opening to have your entire team discuss what it is they actually do. Everyone likes talking about what they accomplish and how they accomplish it. Starting with that can make the daunting task of uncovering the "why" more approachable. Blum describes a gradual narrowing of focus as the team moved through what they do and how they do it.

"Why do we do what we do at the National Gaucher Foundation?" Blum says. "Ultimately, it's because we want to ensure that no Gaucher patient is left behind."

Focusing in on that reason – because no Gaucher patient should be left behind – is exactly the kind of sentiment that will compel the foundation's audience to pay attention. The rare disease often goes ignored, and the foundation's reason for existing is to balance the scales – to advocate for those who might, in fact, be left behind.

Your beliefs power your why

Sinek famously jokes in his talk that Martin Luther King, Jr. didn't call his "I Have a Dream" speech the "I Have a Plan" speech. Sinek's implicit point is that people rallied around King because he had beliefs, and beliefs are a majorly powerful force in decision-making.

For purpose-driven organizations, articulating the belief that powers them is of utmost importance. Beliefs are usually at the heart of purpose-driven organizations, but they are rarely articulated, especially in marketing materials.

Let's look at some examples from big companies and large nonprofit organizations: why does Nike make shoes? The company believes in fitness. Why does Patagonia make outdoor gear the way that it does? Because "…a love of wild and beautiful places demands participation in the fight to save them."

Consider Warby Parker's mission statement. He claims the company "was founded with a rebellious spirit and a lofty objective: to offer designer eyewear at a revolutionary price, while leading the way for socially conscious businesses."

TOMS Shoes mission statement is: "For every pair you purchase, TOMS will give a pair to a child in need. One for one."

Oxfam's mission statement is just five words long: "A just world without poverty." Kiva's is a bit longer: "We envision a world where all people – even in the most remote areas of the globe—hold the power to create opportunity for themselves and others.

And the mission statement for Amnesty International envisions a "world in which every person enjoys all of the human rights enshrined in the Universal Declaration of Human Rights and other international human rights instruments."

To paraphrase Sinek, people don't want to be part of what you do; they want to be part of *why you do it*. They want to do business with people who believe what they believe.

This is why it's important that you are able to clearly and effectively communicate the belief (or beliefs) that informs your organization's reason for existing. Furthermore, revealing your beliefs to your audience, in turn, demonstrates your organization's authenticity.

Your audience doesn't pay attention to product-hawking or service-shilling. They pay attention when real people who sound like them say things that resonate with their experience. Once you're able to do that, you'll attract the kind of loyal, belief-driven partners, customers, and supporters that can build an organization's future.

Big benefits of knowing your why

Better understand your audience and your potential audience
Your audience may have a lot of demographic differences. They may come from different parts of the world. Some might be Boomers and others Millennials. What unites them is their shared belief in your *why*.

Articulating your *why* will allow you to analyze how and why your audience identifies with your mission. And it will make clear who you should reach out to, since it is these people who will share your beliefs. All your connections are based on a shared *why*.

Better team
Not only is your audience made up of people who share your why – your best employees are committed to your vision, too.

"The goal is not just to hire people who need a job but to hire people who believe what you believe," writes Olivia Perek, the inbound marketing strategist at New Breed Marketing. "If you hire people just because they can do a job, they'll work for your money. If you hire people who believe in what you believe, they will work alongside you and help grow your business."

As a purpose-driven organization, this is something you have probably noticed among your team. People who are motivated by the bigger purpose of your organization are the ones who support real growth. This is a residual effect of articulating your *why*.

Better content

Your *why* is at the core of all of your messaging. It is both the most important thing to communicate to your audience and also the belief that undergirds every single story or image you share.

A well-defined *why* will make your content richer, higher quality, and more effective. It will result in a more coherent digital strategy.

Think of your *why* as the foundation on which all your communications are built. A solid *why* supports the growth of all other parts of your digital strategy.

And when it comes time to measure the effectiveness of your digital strategy, the first question you will ask is: has my strategy successfully served my core values and beliefs? Has it helped me achieve my *why?*

What does this process actually look like?

Maga Design, a marketing, communications, and design firm, wants both the "why" and its resulting strategy to feel as tangible as possible to their clients. They work with their client organizations to "co-create" a vision. "By visualizing and mapping a challenge or opportunity space, we have the chance to help drive alignment and consensus around strategy," says Caleb Sexton, senior design strategist at Maga Design.

After it figure out the *why,* Maga Design works to contextualize the concept in an engaging and meaningful way across the client organization. "This can come about in many ways, from communications tools, videos, day-in-the-life scenarios, or wholly built experiences," says Sexton. "For an organization to align their efforts around a shared idea of what must be done to achieve success and gain buy-in, visualizing strategy is a key. It allows team members to feel heard. It gives them a way engage with the process more dynamically."

So get out those markers and huge pieces of paper. There is work to do.

CASE STUDY: SAVE DC'S KIDS

Let's use Save DC's Kids as our case study example that we'll use to demonstrate the ideas of each chapter of this book. This organization doesn't really exist, but we've worked with a whole bunch of organizations with causes just as worthy and a slew of similar challenges, too. So for the purposes of this case study, let's run with Save DC's Kids ("Save") as our hypothetical organizational example.

Save's *why* is simple: children are our future and every child deserves a fair start. (Full disclosure: the organization's *why* was not always this clear. During earlier iterations, other populations were included, such as teenagers. But as time went on, Save determined that investing in children DOES help teens, as well as keeping their mission focused. The organization is actually more successful in helping multiple populations when it just focuses on helping one.)

How does the organization give DC's youth a fair start? By giving kids access to high quality education starting at age three and the services to support the child to ensure success in school. Save does this in three ways:

1. Teacher training
2. Needs-based before and after school care
3. Nutritious meals and snacks

DEFINE YOUR "WHY?"

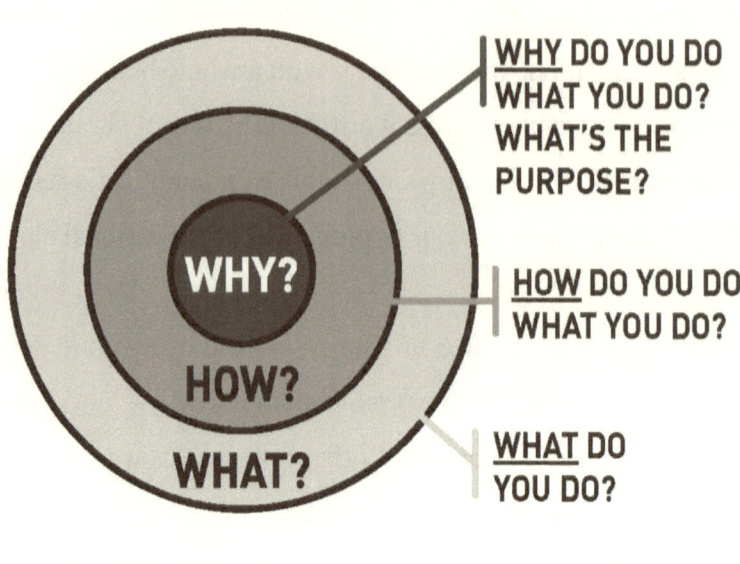

WHY DO YOU DO
WHAT YOU DO?
WHAT'S THE
PURPOSE?

HOW DO YOU DO
WHAT YOU DO?

WHAT DO
YOU DO?

WE BELIEVE...

_____
_____
_____

WE DO THIS BY...

_____
_____
_____

WE PROVIDE...

_____
_____
_____

REFERENCES

Sexton, C. (2017, July 19). Phone interview

Perek, O. (2014, November 04). The Importance of a Why Statement. Retrieved from https://www.newbreedmarketing.com/blog/the-importance-of-a-why-statement

Sinek, S. (2009, September). How great leaders inspire action. Retrieved from https://www.ted.com/talks/simon_sinek_how_great_leaders_inspire_action

CHAPTER 2
CREATE YOUR BRAND STORY

Here's the hard truth: nobody cares about your brand.

On average, people encounter 20,000 brands every day. That's 20,000 brands beginning with the moment a person turns off the iPhone alarm clock and goes to the kitchen to grind Starbucks coffee beans in a Capresso grinder.

These days, asking people to care about your organization is like asking them to identify a single molecule of air as the most important in their day. We've reached Peak Brand, and in this era of inundation, a single tweet announcing a new product isn't enough. You've got to stand out. But how?

Standing out among the 20,000 is the most pressing concern facing brands today. How are you going to grab the attention of your audience? What story are you going to tell that encapsulates your organization? What goes into a good brand story?

Three ingredients for a brand

A good place to start crafting a brand story is by defining your organization.

An organization might be recognized by a colorful logo or a catchy jingle, but that isn't actually what defines the organization for customers. What differentiates and defines an organization in the marketplace is an organization's character. So what constitutes character?

The simplest way to think of it is in terms of these three ingredients, which will ultimately guide you to good storytelling.

1. Brand promise

A brand first and foremost makes a promise. Nike may be memorable because of their iconic "swoosh," but their brand promise – *"to bring inspiration and innovation to every athlete in the world"* – is why Nike diehards love them. Everything Nike does encapsulates that promise, from their inspirational print ads to their clean but edgy website aesthetic to their innovative digital content.

Note that nowhere in the brand promise does Nike mention their products. This can be a powerful move, especially when your brand provides something a lot of other brands also provide. Adidas, Puma, and New Balance also make athletic gear targeting a similar audience. But with Nike's brand promise, they've positioned themselves as the brand that will bring inspiration and innovation to your workout, leaving the other brands to either best them or scramble towards different promises.

In practice: What kind of interaction is your brand promising your audience? What feeling do you always want to leave with them? What experiences will be delivered by engaging with your brand?

2. Brand benefit

Let's stick with Nike. The literal benefit of buying a Nike product is that a customer now owns a pair of running shoes. But the *brand benefit* is something beyond owning the product or using the service. When a person owns a Nike product, she is benefitting from brand association. She is now seen as a serious athlete of the world, someone interested in having the very best gear for the very best workout.

A brand benefit could also be something more tangible. For example, Volvo owners reap the benefits of consistent road safety because the vehicles are known as one of the safest in the world. Those who listen to music on the subway through Beats by Dre headphones are thought of as connoisseurs of high-quality sound. People who carry around the popular (and expensive) bkr glass water bottles show they care about the environment and personal health without forgoing luxury. In each of these examples, the brand has made a promise to deliver an experience, and once the consumer has that experience, the benefit is apparent. The benefit is what keeps them coming back.

In practice: What will your audience get from engaging with your brand? I don't mean what products or services does she get, but what kind of association does she benefit from, whether it's a feeling, a reputation, or a more tangible benefit? For example, if she makes a donation to your cause, what is the impact she will make? What is the return on her investment? How do you want her to feel after interacting with your organization?

3. Brand story

And finally, we land at your brand story: that which communicates the *promise* and *benefit* in the form of a narrative. While you may not end up communicating your brand story through video – though I recommend you do – it's helpful to think of it as a trailer. Trailers for films don't tell you information such as who are the stars or what is the subject. Learning those facts would be not only boring but unrelated to why you want to go see the film. Instead, a trailer shows you the film in a mini-story version, in order to elicit an emotional experience that stays with you and compels you to see the film when it's released.

Brand stories work similarly: the story you tell helps your audience identify with your brand. For purpose-driven organizations, your brand story is the most powerful expression of who you are and the impact you have on the world.

Staying with the Nike example, let's look at what the series of ads for Nike Women released in 2015. In one ad, a woman tries a spin class for the first time, another struggles in a yoga class, while another runs in a road race, but is slower than other runners. But each woman perseveres; the woman in the spin class gets into the zone, the woman in the yoga class is able to accomplish a difficult pose, and the runner crosses the finish line. The ad could have *told* the audience the information they needed to know by simply displaying their new line of sportswear for women. But instead, the ad tells a story -- a unique, relatable story -- from the perspective of a consumer who is inspirational. At the beginning of the ad, the women in the story are unsure, doubtful, and cynical. By the end, they are believers, both strong and proud. The ad *shows* the women benefitting from the brand promise. And that is exactly what the consumer gets from buying a pair of Nike Women leggings: the promise of experiencing athletic inspiration, and the benefit of association with respected peers.

*In practice: Remember to **show, don't tell**. Nowhere in that Nike ad is the gear mentioned. When you watch it, you don't feel like someone is trying to sell you something. Good brand stories don't tell the audience about products or services; they show them in action, from the perspective of the individual, in an emotionally compelling story.*

Why does brand storytelling work?

You need to look no further than the entertainment industry to know that stories sell. Every year, we spend millions upon millions of dollars to go see films that tell us good stories. We crave the emotional experience of being told a story, and brands are wise to take a cue. In an age where the market is inundated with brands clamoring for customer attention, the only tactic that consistently cuts through is telling resonant stories.

The power of storytelling isn't an idea limited to marketers, either. Science backs us up. Using research reported in the *New York Times,* Neil Patel wrote about the science of storytelling at KISSmetrics: "The human brain responds to the descriptive power of stories in deeply affecting ways, influencing both the sensory and motor cortex. To read a story is to feel an experience and to synchronize our minds with the subject of the story."

In short, stories have power because users attach the emotional experience they have when watching the story to the brand telling it. They trust the brand because the experience they've had was real. Tell a good story, and you'll leave an emotional imprint on someone that's hard to shake.

How do you know what story to tell?

Brand stories aren't ads or marketing pitches. Brand stories are stories, and should be thought of in that way. There are three key steps that are essential for every organization invested in stories: perspective, plot, and permutation.

Step 1: Find your perspective

You can't tell a story without a main character. Who will be yours? For brands that are selling a product, storytelling is often told best from the customer's perspective, showing a successful brand interaction in a unique way. For purpose-drive organizations that provide a service, it is generally more useful to tell a story from the perspective of the community being served.

In either case, it's useful to think in terms of user personas. (As a reminder: a user persona is a representation of the behavior and goals of a hypothesized group of users. Most often, personas are created using data collected from interviews with users.) If you're selling a product, is there a persona that lends itself more to storytelling? If you're a purpose-driven organization, what story about your service will resonate with one of your user personas? You want your audience to identify with your story, because identification engenders trust. They should see themselves in your story – any good narrative always starts with them.

Step 2: Draft a plot

Storytelling *is* plot, and writing yours is going to be the most important step in the process. Remember brand promise and brand benefit? They are what the user expects in a brand interaction and what she gets out of it. Your plot should carry this out, either by showing a user benefitting from the brand promise, or by showing the brand promise carried out in the served community.

Don't be afraid to think in storyboard form, whether or not you end up making a video version of it. Your plot should be as easy to follow as a storyboard, and it'll help you hit the main pivot points. Where does it begin and where does it end up? How is the experience changing for the main character and what emotional note does the story hit at the conclusion?

Step 3: Think in permutations

Now that you have a story, how will you tell it? Does it only exist in video form? If so, you might be in trouble, because there are only so many times you can link to that video. The half-life of a single piece of content isn't very long, but it doesn't have to be that way. You can extend it by making sure you are able to tell your brand story in various iterations on various social channels.

A good brand story is flexible enough to live on many communication channels. Beautiful still photos from the story have appropriate copy for Instagram. The story leads to audience questions or calls-to-action on Twitter and Facebook. Pieces of the story are bite-sized shareable content for Twitter. A story hashtag encourages user-generated content. You've spent all this time creating a brand story. You might as well make sure you are able to tell it again and again.

What do good digital brand stories look like?

A fantastic example of purpose-driven brand storytelling that successfully elicits an emotional response is a video by Water Is Life, in which a four-year-old Kenyan boy named Nkaitole, who has never left his village, makes a bucket list that Water for Life helps him to fulfill. (At the beginning, the audience is informed that one in five children like Nkaitole will not see their fifth birthday.) In riveting visuals, we see Nkaitole fly in an airplane, play soccer in the National Stadium, see the ocean, and get his first kiss. The images are uplifting and joyful. Nkaitole's awe shows on his face. The world, and the experienced possibilities for us all, seems rich with beauty. A title card at the end of the video informs the audience that unsafe drinking water is the leading cause of death of children under five.

Water Is Life is a nonprofit dedicated to providing clean water for communities around the world and in their video they clearly demonstrate what the organization does and *why* they do it – through a very specific community perspective, along a linear storyline, with an extremely positive emotional ending. The result is nothing less than compelling.

Takeaway: An authentic inspirational story can be the most memorable story you'll tell, especially in a world where companies can be seen as cheaply tugging at heartstrings. Don't shy away from the profound, as long as it aligns with your brand promise.

GoPro's tagline is "Be a Hero," and it's often interpreted by users in reference to extreme sports. GoPro users are frequently the heroes of their own YouTube videos that include base jumping stunts or snowboarding tricks. But the most recent viral GoPro video has nothing to do with sports. In this video, the brand story is narrated literally by a fireman as he saves a kitten from a burned out house. The video shows images of a dark interior as the fireman searches the house, then he finds a kitten lying on the floor, unresponsive. He carries the kitten out of the house and revives it with oxygen and water.

There's no grand narrative to the video – in fact, there is no speaking at all – but it does very clearly show the product in action, in an unexpected, emotional way. Most importantly, a real GoPro customer – someone who other customers would identify with and therefore trust – is using the product himself.

Takeaway: Your brand story can and should engender trust. One way to do that is to clearly show the product or service in use by a real-life customer. The kind of emotional experience that your audience has with that person's story is what will produce a lasting sense of trust in your organization.

All too commonly organizations rely on lists of facts and statistics to do the persuasive work for them: "We feed 300 families living under the poverty line in the metro area" or "Forty-four percent of children are missing one meal a day." Percentages and facts are good for snackable social content, but they aren't memorable. They might be memorable if they're embedded in a brand story, but the bottom line is that stories are inherently more interesting than facts. One brand that really gets this is Google. While they could rely on stats—the vast numbers of people across the world who use the search engine—to state their impact, they don't.

Instead, they tell stories. In an ad called "Google Search: Reunion," two boyhood friends who were separated by the partition of India and Pakistan are reunited by the efforts of a granddaughter with help from Google. The granddaughter uses Google to input her grandfather's boyhood recollections to find his lost friend. Then she uses Google to organize his visit to India. She even uses Google to make sure she is on time to pick up her grandfather's friend from the airport. The ad closes with the grandfather opening the door and seeing his friend, who he hasn't seen in more than 50 years. He recognizes him and the two men embrace.

The ad cleverly tells an emotional story that hinges on the use of Google. Instead of being told about the product, we are seeing it in action.

Takeaway: People don't connect to stats as much as they do to personal stories. They can't empathize with something without seeing it. They can't understand impact without feeling it. Get out of your facts-and-figures comfort zone. After all, purpose-driven organizations often deal in people, not numbers.

Hack: use video to tell your brand story

Using video is an excellent way to tell your brand story. It will help you steer clear of the dry facts and statistics that you might usually lean on to validate your organization. It also forces you to focus on the visuals – those details that constitute a compelling narrative. The value of a video brand story is really this: it's the most immediate way to get your audience to *feel* something.

Why does it matter if they feel something? Because emotion drives engagement. Emotion drives financial decisions, social shares, and loyalty. Put that way, investment in a top-quality digital video to tell your brand story seems like a sound investment. But you don't have to invest a lot of money these days to make – and measure – a great video: not with Vimeo, vlogging cameras, YouTube, Instagram, and the number of sophisticated video analytics platforms popping up.

Don't forget to focus on telling a story. Focus on the narrative, including a beginning, middle, and end. Make the story small and personal, even if what you do is global and big picture. Favor authenticity over grandstanding, and create the video as a trailer not necessarily for what your organization does, but what it believes.

Offer a unique series

Ever wonder how YouTube stars have so many subscribers? Aside from a variety of natural talents, it's this: consistency. Each successful YouTuber has an angle, whether it's beauty guru, parenting, comedy, or world travel. And each star has a perspective, and they offer that perspective on a regular basis – in what is known as a channel, but what is really a series.

Think of a video content strategy as something that offers your perspective – regularly and consistently – in different episodes. This gives you the benefit of thinking about your strategy in the long term, while zeroing in on the narrative of each particular episode of your series.

If your organization helps a community of people, one video strategy could be a monthly feature on a person or family involved. Interview them or let them tell their own story of personal experience with your organization. If your organization advocates for a cause, consider an educational series. If you are dealing with the environment, highlight a different part of the world in your video series, and tell a compelling story about what your organization does or wants to do there. If you are an organization that, for example, wants to help young girls succeed at math and science, perhaps put those young girls in front of the camera to give a math or science lesson.

The idea behind the series is to put a face to your organization and a story to your cause. If you know the driving emotion behind your cause, telling the stories that capture an audience won't be far behind.

Pull back the curtain

There is perhaps nothing an audience loves more than exclusivity. If you can't offer exclusive discounts, offer exclusive access. One way to do this is to go behind-the-scenes of your organization, or of communities your organization has relationships with. Show what makes your organization tick by featuring the people or processes that work for it. The benefit of this is twofold: showing the gears of your organization helps validate what you do, while sharing the behind-the-scenes stories provides emotional value for your audience.

One way to go behind-the-scenes is to showcase your company culture. If you have a tradition in your office that might be interesting to outsiders, tell a story about what you do and why it's important. Do members of your staff have expertise or back stories to share? It always helps emotional engagement to show the faces of the people who actually do the work. Don't shroud your CEO or top-level executives in mystery; in the days of digital transparency, it's expected that your entire team be available, especially on social media. Bottom line: a charming staff member with a good story can go a long way in a video.

Telling a brand story is like telling a love story. It's the most powerful digital marketing tool any organization has, and it's particularly powerful for purpose-driven organizations, where the tangible goal is more than just making a profit. It's building an audience, a community, ambassadors, fans, and advocates. It might even draw in a few fanatics.

A few extra storytelling ideas

Have fun: This is your time to have fun with your digital content. People respond to personality, and storytelling is your moment to showcase your brand personality. Brand storytelling isn't the time to think inside the box.

Inspire: Even if you don't go the inspirational route in your regular marketing copy, think about it for brand storytelling. Airbnb, a brand not often associated with inspirational messaging, put together an excellent animated digital video – "Wall and Chain: A Story of Breaking Down Walls" – perhaps taking a cue from Google. The story is about Jörg, a Berlin Wall guard at the height of the Cold War. He carries the experience of guarding the wall with him through his life, even after the Cold War ends and his family leaves Germany, but when he returns to Berlin years later, his Airbnb host is the guard who worked on the opposite side of the wall from him. Now the former enemy welcomes him as a friend. "And after that things were better for my father," says the narrator, Jörg's daughter.

In the ad, AirBnB really nailed the tone, used innovative visuals, including global touchpoints, and a moving storyline in an inspirational reinterpretation of their "Belong Anywhere" tagline.

Do it yourself (DIY): If you can't afford to hire actors or other high cost services, consider using the staff you already have to speak as brand ambassadors, to tell your brand story through their eyes. Reach out to satisfied clients that could give compelling testimonials, or influencers who might be interested in doing some *gratis* work with a charitable organization.

Be authentic: Be strategic with your storytelling, but most of all, be your most authentic self. Your audience can sense trying too hard a mile away. You can always go back to your "why" as discussed in the previous chapter, to zero in on the authentic reason your organization exists. That should inspire the story you tell.

CASE STUDY: SAVE DC'S KIDS

BRAND STORY

After three years of early childhood education teaching in one of DC's underserved communities, Tricia Papsdorf decided that she needed to do more. She saw parents who had high hopes for their kids and a broken system that failed them. She saw teachers who were burned out and in need of extra support. Tricia saw rising crime rates in communities surrounding the school where she taught and alarming dropout rates, too. And she saw Andre, a sweet four-year old with a love of dinosaurs and dancing. Tricia knew that she couldn't let Andre, his parents, or her fellow teachers down given the classroom overcrowding and glaring lack of wrap-around services needed to set DC's little ones up for success.

Inspired by Nelson Mandela's famous quote, "Education is the most powerful weapon which you can use to change the world," Tricia gathered a group of parents, teachers, neighbors, and a former grad school professor around her dining room table. That was August 1996 and the temperatures outside were in the triple digits. Tricia's husband put some burgers on the grill and before dessert was served, Save DC's Kids was born.

For the first few years of Save's existence, the organization had trouble attracting board members with high giving potential or major clout within the DC community. Tricia brought in a board development consultant to help shore things up and thankfully that time has ended and the Save board is robust and strong. Today, Save boasts a board composed of a DC Councilwoman, three DC public school teachers, two local philanthropists, and several parents.

The recession hit Save DC's Kids hard as both DC Public School budgets were being cut while individual philanthropy was declining too. Luckily, Save has always operated with a lean staffing model and the decreased funds didn't necessitate any layoffs.

In 2016, over 80 percent of the organization's funding came from individuals and foundations in the DC metro area. The same year, Save trained over 5,000 teachers, provided 13,321 meals and snacks for DC's youth and more than 10,000 hours of before and after care.

Tone and voice:

As an organization, Save decided on an informal tone with a nod to the gravity of the work that they're trying to accomplish. This decision was made after some trial and error with a tone that was very child centered. Save soon realized that although they were talking ABOUT kids, they were not talking to kids and their tone needed to match their audience as opposed to their target constituency. The organization's paramount goal is to tug at the heartstrings of potential donors, so a good dose of personal stories and quotes are used (rather than peppering content with too many statistics). The organizational voice is smart yet serious, mostly conversational with a dash of wonky (we are in DC!).

CREATE YOUR BRAND STORY

ACT 1

ACT 2

ACT 3

BRAND PROMISE:

REFERENCES

Patel, N. (2015). How to Create an Authentic Brand Story that Actually Improves Trust. Retrieved from https://blog.kissmetrics.com/create-authentic-brand-story/

CHAPTER 3
SET YOUR GOALS

There is no athletic game on earth that doesn't have clear goals that signify a win (well, except maybe cricket) – and yet, so many organizations move forward with digital strategies before clearly defining the main goals. This undoubtedly leads to major fumbling, and even if there is a win, you have no documented way of how you got there.

I understand why goal setting is often overlooked. The last decade has seen a mass rush for every organization to have a digital plan. A desire to be part of the digital space can (wrongly) trump the process of careful strategizing. Not to mention that social media has so many moving parts that figuring out where to focus can be difficult. The unromantic process of goal setting is easily overshadowed.

A recent article by John Rampton in Forbes explores how a lack of goal setting is a common reason for the failure of social media efforts.

He writes, "Just because you're on Facebook, Twitter, LinkedIn, or Pinterest doesn't guarantee success. Even if you have a decent amount of fans, likes, or followers, it doesn't mean that your social media strategy is working. If you're not generating conversations or new subscribers, or making any money, then whatever you're doing has failed."

Rampton names several qualities that a successful social media effort should include:

a) Matching your social media efforts to your core values as an organization. You want to have the right goals for your core values.

b) Making sure your social media efforts are consistent across time. You can't take breaks from social media; if you do, you will lose your audience. When setting goals, keep in mind that you'll need to be able to do your tasks consistently. What resources will you need to do so?

c) Understanding the differences between the social media platforms. Figuring out where your audience is, and then using your knowledge of the platform to communicate as clearly as you can with your audience. Learning will be an intrinsic part of meeting your goals.

d) Providing something unique in your content. Figuring out how you are a little different from other organizations and how to capitalize on that difference should be a goal.

e) Listening and conversing on social media. Don't just broad-cast. Listening is often overlooked, but it should also be a goal.

f) Measuring your results. This is the only way you can figure out if you are meeting your goals.

When you are putting together your goals, try to address these concerns. Make sure that your goals match your core values. A goal should only be a goal if it really matters.

The goal setting process

In the same way that archers wouldn't let an arrow fly without knowing where they were aiming, a digital strategy can't get off the ground without a set of tangible goals. A lot of organizations go from creating a brand story to drafting audience journey maps, but skipping the goal setting part of the process is skipping the part that informs every other element of the campaign execution.

Be S.M.A.R.T.

There are lots of acronyms that can guide you through goal setting, but the one I find most useful is S.M.A.R.T. Your goals for any digital campaign should be:

- Specific
- Measurable
- Attainable
- Relevant
- Time-bound

SPECIFIC

If you toss the ball in the general direction of the net, it's good, but probably not good enough to score. The same goes for making your digital strategy goals specific. If you have a specific target in mind, the team always has a set of objectives to work towards, and the chances of campaign success increase. Specific goal setting increases the consistency of your team's actions, and the clarity of decision-making.

Beware of setting goals that are too lofty, especially if a single digital campaign can't achieve it. Don't confuse the goals of your organization (which are often more visionary) with the goals of your campaign. While they should be related to each other (see "Relevant," below), campaign goals should be very specific to the activities of the campaign.

Bad example: This Facebook advertising campaign promoting our annual gala will contribute to our goals to end world hunger.

Good example: The two goals of promoting the video through a three-month Facebook advertising campaign are to 1) sell at least 100 tickets to the annual gala, and 2) add 250 new e-mail addresses to our list.

MEASURABLE

Scores are measured in numbers, not feelings, and the same goes for your digital strategy goals. Metrics have been the buzzword of the last few years, and for good reason. The C-Suite speaks in numbers: the marketing department must communicate results in terms of the bottom line. If you want the higher-ups to invest resources in your campaign, you have to prove the campaign's worthiness, and that proof is in the metrics.

But having measurable goals is also good for the digital strategy itself. If you can measure something, you're able to determine the quality of its success. The worst way to approach a digital strategy is to feel your way through it. If you set a specific goal that is measurable in the digital space, you will have something to look to when determining whether the campaign was a win or a loss. Otherwise, you'll be shooting in the dark.

A side note about sentiment: if your goal is to build positive audience sentiment, be careful. There are a few pricey platforms out there that measure sentiment – or you can do it on your own through keyword measurement – but because the way people speak online is so particular and nuanced, measuring sentiment is going to be a difficult task.

Bad example: This campaign will increase brand awareness.

Good example: We will determine how much this campaign increased brand awareness by measuring Facebook video shares and traffic to the landing page, and then compare that to the results of last quarter's campaign.

ATTAINABLE

Good goals stretch your capability beyond what you normally do – that is why they are goals, not tasks. But goals should not be so out of reach that you set yourself up for failure. Finding the sweet spot between a goal that is aspirational and a goal that leaves you in the status quo is an important step.

Knowing what's attainable means knowing your resources. What kind of money are you allocating for this campaign? How many staff will be dedicated to it and how much of their time will be spent on this particular project?

And you guessed it: attainable goals are directly linked to measurable goals. When you start putting goals in terms of metrics, you'll very quickly be able to see if they're attainable or not.

Bad example: The goal of this Q1 Twitter strategy is to emerge as a thought leader in global nonprofits.

Good example: By the end of Q1, this Twitter strategy will result in a 25 percent increase in followers, a 30 percent increase in re-tweets, and 50 percent more traffic driven to the site.

RELEVANT

Sure, it would be cool to have 500,000 Twitter followers. But is that relevant for your larger business objectives? If you're trying to drum up large donations from major philanthropic organizations, will 500,000 Twitter followers help?

It might, but it certainly wouldn't be the first place to go. However, if you're trying to gather signatures to pass legislation about housing and homelessness, then yes, a major Twitter following will probably help.

The point here is not to rush to a social strategy without knowing how it's going to be relevant for your particular organization. Every organization – even nonprofits – should have business objectives, and a digital strategy should serve those objectives. So don't go after millennials on Snapchat if your greater mission wouldn't be helped by engaging millennials (or, for that matter, if your organization's content doesn't work on Snapchat.) Bottom line: don't dunk your ball in the wrong net.

Bad example: Our foundation, which gathers donations to provide housing in rural India, will invest in an influencer partnership with a YouTuber, whose audience is mainly people between 14 and 24.

Good example: Our foundation's mission – to raise awareness of and funds to support efforts to empower women and girls in rural areas of the globe – will be served by a partnership with a specific YouTuber, whose audience is mainly women between 16 and 28, and will include a call-to-action to share a video, use the hashtag, and donate what they can.

TIME-BOUND

Every game has a clock that runs out, and so should your digital strategy. No one wants to deal with a sprawling, vaguely purposeful campaign, which is what happens when a strategy goes unchecked without an end in sight. Set a very specific time stamp on your goal – say, 18 months – with benchmark goals along the way. This way, you will know how to measure a win. The benchmarks can serve as breathing points where you can do mini-evaluations and change course if needed. Of course, if your goals are specific and measurable, evaluation will be a cinch.

Bad example: Over the next two years, this campaign will work towards raising brand awareness.

Good example: We will create one three-minute video every three months following the specific narrative of a young girl in Kenya, and how she was helped by the foundation's programs. At the end of each three-month period, we expect video shares on social media to be up by 30 percent and conversions to increase by 10 percent, and a ticket sales benchmark working towards the gala at the end of the year, which is at the end of our 18-month video marketing campaign.

Different Ways to Be S.M.A.R.T.

Other organizations arrange these steps in different ways. Some use M.A.R.S.T, starting with making sure their goals are measurable, so that hard numbers are the foundation of every action. However, if you decide it's best to prioritize these steps, it will be a process that will set you up for success down the line.

S.M.A.R.T. is only one goal setting strategy among many, but most are based on similar ideas. In the 1960s, Drs. Edwin Locke and Gary Latham researched how goals and feedback motivate employees in businesses. Locke and Latham encouraged making goals clear and specific. According to an article by Kevan Lee at Buffer, Locke discovered that rather than telling subjects to "do your best," telling them to "try to beat your best time" led to better results. Indeed, "specific and challenging goals led to higher performance 90 percent of the time," according to Lee. Locke and Latham also champion gathering feedback or, in other words, measuring one's progress and results.

The two ideas that are novel to Locke and Latham are getting a team to commit to a goal by including them in the goal setting process and reducing complexity when possible. Just like a diet is easier to stick to when it's simple, goals are easier to attain when they are less complex. Overly complex goals negatively impact morale, productivity, and motivation.

According to Lee, Google uses a goal setting process that breaks goals down into objectives and key results. The objectives are broad goals that are often not measurable. The key objectives break that broad goal down into specific and measurable parts. One might think of the objectives as the grand "what," and the key results as the "how."

There are many other goal setting systems, but they tend to share the attributes of those mentioned already. Some emphasize sharing goal setting and the results of one's efforts with a whole team, both to keep a team focused and to provide accountability.

Carter Hostelley, CEO of Leadtail, has made a list of the categories of goals appropriate for social media campaigns:

1. Activity-based goals: goals related to the number of blog posts per month, tweets per day and status updates per week that you and your team can do.

2. Audience-building goals: goals related to the number of email subscribers, website visitors, and followers on Facebook, LinkedIn, Twitter, etc.

3. Engagement goals: goals related to the social reach of your content, retweets, mentions, likes and comments. "Also establish with which and how many industry influencers you're engaging," writes Hostelley.

4. ROI goals: goals related to donations, signing up for services, tickets to fundraising galas, etc.

Whichever goal setting strategy you use, they are backed up by the same science. Lee mentions a research finding that shows a 33 percent increase in the completion of goals among people who write their goals down, create an action plan, and share their goals with a friend. "These people achieved 76 percent of their goals by having a specific goal-setting strategy," writes Lee.

The danger of goal drift

Like mission drift, when an organization's objectives gradually change, goal drift is when goals change mid-stream in a manner that makes them harder to achieve. This is most common when a project is long and complex. Often the larger goals are kept the same, but the smaller goals are adjusted, to the detriment of the larger goal. We all know someone with an unfinished book in a box in their closet. Most of us have had a gym membership that we hardly used despite our initial best intentions.

"A friend who wanted to start a web-based business originally aimed for launch six months after he began work with his website designers," says Sierra Bellows, a social media marketing professional. "But two years later, the business had not yet launched despite the fact that my friend was working very long hours and putting his best effort toward the business. He's a smart guy and capable."

Bellows says that the problem was goal drift. As the entrepreneur worked, his goals changed; indeed, they grew more complex and ambitious. "Part of the problem was that he is a perfectionist and he wanted everything to be perfect before he launched," Bellows explains. "Also the job was big and he wasn't able to divide it into smaller, attainable sub-goals before he started."

We all know the aphorism, "perfect is the enemy of good." Perfection is also unattainable. So being realistic about what can be achieved and having a good understanding of the needs of the project before you start makes your chances of success much higher.

There are other reasons for goal drift, such as fear of failure or saving face. Sometimes it can be helpful to be flexible enough to allow for your goals to change when your circumstances change. Certainly, if your metrics suggest that a changed goal would serve your organizations better, listen to your metrics. But be wary of whether goal drift is hurting or helping you.

"I also think that because my friend was the sole proprietor in his business venture, he didn't have anyone to call him on his missed deadlines. He wasn't accountable to anyone but himself," says Bellows. When you tell someone else your goals, or if you share common goals with a team, it will be easier to stick to them, even when the going gets tough.

Case Study: Save DC's Kids

S.M.A.R.T. GOALS

In the next 12 months, the organization aims to:

1. Gain 10,000 new social media followers/email house file members (we'll talk more about which online marketing channels matter to Save and why in the Key Channels case study)
2. Process online donations from 1,000 supporters

3. Welcome 100 new super volunteers (aka Save Stars) to their ranks. (Save Stars are like community ambassadors; they're trained on organizational messaging and serve as volunteer grassroots organizers to grow Save's DC donor and activist base.)

Save staff consulted several sources when coming up with these numbers. First, they were throwing around numbers that were about triple the ones mentioned above. This was easy to do because board members and potential foundations were pushing Save to grow VERY big VERY fast with their enhanced online presence.

This scared the Save Director of Development, Susan, so she looked at these metrics for the past few years to inform realistic goals for next year. Then, she connected with a digital strategist to ensure their numbers were attainable and that they had a plan to meet their goals. Lastly, the Save development team secured funding from a major donor to fund part of the expenses associated with this expanded marketing and fundraising strategy. In order to secure the funds, the organization committed to meeting these goals. The pressure is on!

DEFINE YOUR GOALS

GOAL #1

- [ ] **S**PECIFIC
- [ ] **M**EASURABLE
- [ ] **A**TTAINABLE
- [ ] **R**ELEVANT
- [ ] **T**IME-BOUND

GOAL #2

- [ ] **S**PECIFIC
- [ ] **M**EASURABLE
- [ ] **A**TTAINABLE
- [ ] **R**ELEVANT
- [ ] **T**IME-BOUND

GOAL #3

- [ ] **S**PECIFIC
- [ ] **M**EASURABLE
- [ ] **A**TTAINABLE
- [ ] **R**ELEVANT
- [ ] **T**IME-BOUND

GOAL #4

- [ ] **S**PECIFIC
- [ ] **M**EASURABLE
- [ ] **A**TTAINABLE
- [ ] **R**ELEVANT
- [ ] **T**IME-BOUND

REFERENCES

Bellows, S. (2017, June 22). Phone interview

Hostelley, C. (2014, July 05). How to Set Social Media Marketing Goals. Retrieved from https://leadtail.com/b2b-social-media-marketing/set-social-media-marketing-goals/

Lee, K. (2017, January 16). 7 Essential Strategies to Set Social Media Goals. Retrieved from https://blog.bufferapp.com/goal-setting-strategies

Rampton, J. (2014, April 22). Why Most Social Media Strategies Fail. Retrieved from https://www.forbes.com/sites/johnrampton/2014/04/22/why-most-social-media-strategies-fail/#2dfb34993a9b

CHAPTER 4
BUILD AUDIENCE PERSONAS

"We need to stop *interrupting* what people are interested in and *be* what people are interested in," writes Craig Davis, Founder of Brandkarma. But first, you must find out what it is that your people are interested in.

Who are you trying to communicate with? What do you know about what these people need or want? The audience persona answers these questions and allows you to target the specifics for the demographics you want to reach.

There is a rumor that at Amazon, Jeff Bezos has an empty chair at meetings to stand in for the customer because decisions should be made with the customer at front of mind. Creating personas is a similar act, only it fills in the details about your customers or your audience. It fills the empty chair.

What is a persona?

"Personas are a method of market segmentation wherein we collect a combination of qualitative and quantitative data to build archetypes of the members of our target audience. In other words we take data to tell a predictive story about our users based on past behaviors and attributes."

- From "Personas: The Art and Science of Understanding the Person Behind the Visit" on Moz.com

"A persona is a full profile of your customer – everything relevant you could possibly want to know about him or her. A persona is not a real person, or someone you know. When you create personas, you want to imagine who these people are, what they care about, and questions they have when they encounter your content. Personas are shared tools to create composites of the real people who interact with our content on a daily basis."

- Ahava Leibtag in her book, "The Digital Crown: Winning at Content on the Web."

Why you need personas

In social media marketing, specificity and personalization matter. Your digital audience is inundated with brand messaging that is trying to reach as many people as possible and, in doing so, becomes watered down and bland. Consumers don't generally respond in a substantive way to a brand message that doesn't have a personal element; they respond when a brand message resonates with them, and in order to resonate with someone, you need to really understand who they are.

"If you don't know who the audience is, how do you get into their heads?" asks Ahava Leibtag of Aha Media Group. "Personas give the writer or the designer empathy for their audience. Personas are like characters in stories: you understand the story through empathy with them. You inhabit their worldview."

Audience personas help you understand who it is that you're speaking to. In developing audience personas, you discover what their unstated needs and desires are, and the places in their lives where your organization might be a natural fit. This helps you understand not only 1) who to target, but 2) how to craft content that is tailored to specific audiences and channels.

How to create personas

Gather audience information

Audience personas don't materialize out of thin air. To create personas, you can do things like conduct audience interviews or perform an organizational audit.

The best possible path to conduct audience research is to interview your audience. If you can speak directly to them, do so. This could happen in many different forms. If you send out regular email blasts, there isn't a reason one of them can't be a nicely-worded survey prompt. Think about any time you've completed a survey and why. Was it because the survey promised to be short? Was it well-designed? Because the "ask" was authentic and well-written?

If you have form fields on your website that users must complete before going further, collect that data. This could give you information about company size, revenue range, pain points, and more.

Well-designed gamified surveys are also an option. Incentivize users to complete a survey with a giveaway or by making it fun to complete, like a game. Don't forget that you can also simply call up current clients and ask them a few questions to clarify your research. Clients that understand that you're only trying to better serve them will likely give you five minutes of their day.

Organizational audits are fantastic supplements to direct client interviews. The key here is to engage people and departments across your organization, particularly those in the sales department (who can often be strangely siloed from marketers). Because members of your sales department talk to your audience daily, it's important to leverage their knowledge when crafting personas. What complaints do they often encounter? What language do they use that accomplishes the most conversions? When are their sales the most successful? What profiles can they provide about your current clients?

Make sure you gather information that is specific to your mission. If you are a foundation that deals with education, you'll want to gather info about whether your audience includes teachers, students, administrators, policymakers, or textbook publishers. Kevan Lee on the Buffer Social blog writes, "An Internet news company would require different customer information than a medical supply company, and a persona built for a buying funnel might look different than one built for a blog."

Your website analytics are a great place to get information to build your personas. "Inside your analytics, you can see where your visitors came from, what keywords they used to find you, and how long they spent once they arrived," writes Lee. This data can reveal the desires that led your audience to you, as well as the tools they used.

Listen in on social media to learn about your audience and potential audience. What kind of questions are people asking about your product or your cause on Twitter, Facebook, or LinkedIn? There are a lot of complaints on social media; use them to figure out what kind of problems your audience has.

Crafting the personas

A persona is created from a mix of data and educated assumptions about your audience. The basic information is relatively easy to get: where your audience lives, their job titles, median age, and main issues. But can you answer the following questions?

- What are their online habits?
- What are their core beliefs?
- What do they love most about their job?
- What are they reading?
- What are they learning?
- Who are they following?
- Who inspires them?
- Where are they traveling?
- What are they investing in?
- What products do they use?
- Who are their friends?
- What's on their bucket list?

A complete persona involves these questions, because what you're trying to find out is not only how you can meet their business needs, but how what you do fits into areas of their lives that inform all of their actions. For example, if you are looking to target different kinds of donors, do you know how your marketing messages could be aligned with the kind of inspiration they like to get from TED Talks?

"Personas breathe real life into your audience so you don't fall into the trap of depersonalizing your customers by thinking of them as users, rather than considering real flesh-and-blood people," writes Leibtag. "Personas help all content creators focus on the customer, making their needs, worries and responsibilities foremost, rather than our own."

Ideally, you will write three to four brand personas for different segments of your audience. You might have separate personas for advocates, volunteers, grant makers and foundations, and donors. Within those personas, you might have further segmentations. Are you targeting both millennial donors and high dollar donors? Will your cause resonate more with the women who tend to make those kinds of financial decisions for their households?

It might seem like your audience can't be divided into just a few personas because their demographic information is too varied. But instead of being distracted by age or income, think about personas as being defined by behavior and motivation. What matters most in creating a persona is what people do and why they do it. "Your audience could have hundreds of different personal characteristics: What unites them makes them one persona, or archetype, even though they may share no other demographic identifiers," writes Leibtag. A boomer who loves computers and a teen addicted to texting might belong to the same persona, even though their demographics are a mismatch.

Quick Tip: Personas don't have to be designed in a super fancy way – as long as the key information is clear. But there are some great online tools to help you such as Xtensio's User Persona Creator.

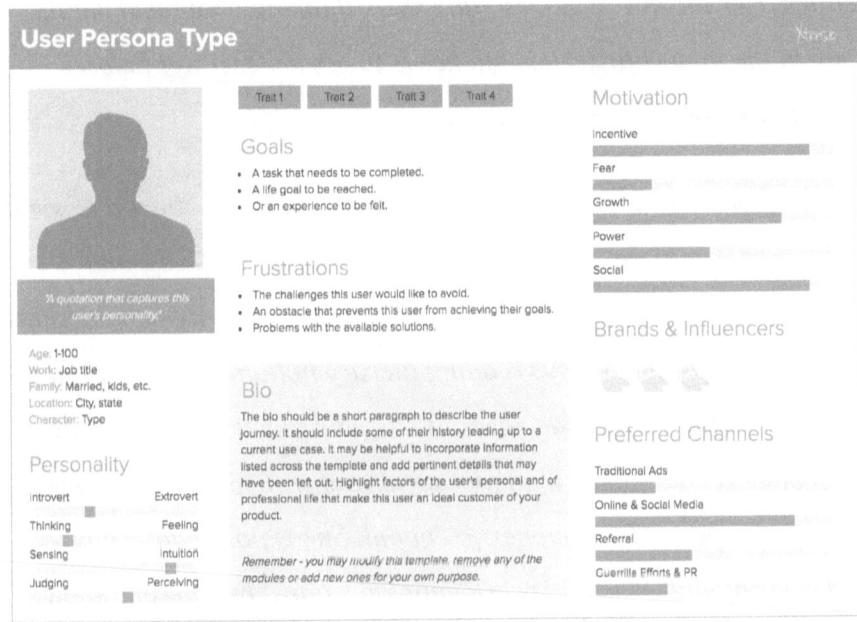

Source: Xtensio.com

An example of a brand persona

Here is an example of a persona for a nonprofit that curates after school programs for youth in at-risk neighborhoods focused on cooking and food education.

AMELIA "THE MILLENNIAL INTERN"

Amelia works an office job in the DC area after graduating from school with a liberal arts education. She is competent and intelligent, but under-used at her office and sees no upward mobility. Amelia holds values from her college experience and her liberal peers about affecting large-scale change in your community through small-scale actions. Her income is modest, and she's thinking about making the jump to the nonprofit sector, but needs to get her feet wet before committing and to gain experience.

She is 25-years old, single, and lives with roommates. Amelia is social media-savvy, majored in English and minored in Business, and depends partially on financial support from her parents, scholarships, and fellowships. She enjoys reading literary fiction and poetry, binge-watching Netflix, 10K road races in DC, and pub trivia. When she has extra money, she spends it on nice meals out with her friends, but mostly she doesn't have money to eat out. She is politically engaged, and votes in midterms and presidential elections, but doesn't know much about local politics. Amelia likes kids, but has no reason to engage with them on a regular basis.

Goals:

- *Financial security with a job that actually makes a difference.*
- *To be engaged in and settled in a community, but to also have upward mobility at a job.*

- *To use her millennial experience with digital media in her work.*

Worries:

- *That she doesn't have enough experience to make the jump.*
- *That she won't find a job that truly engages her and uses all her skills.*
- *That she's chosen the wrong path post-graduation.*

Main sources of entertainment and information:

- *Facebook and Snapchat*
- *YouTube influencers*
- *Refinery 29*
- The New York Times *and* Slate
- *Friends at other nonprofits*

How to use the persona

Once everyone on your marketing team understands what kind of life Amelia lives, her past experience, and what she wants, you can begin to alter your current content or create content that targets her specifically.

An important element to figure out via your personas is where to push your content, or which channels you should be creating content for. For example, a useful move here would be Facebook ads targeted at recent college graduates in the DC area who likes *The New York*

Times. Another option would be to consider leveraging a local influencer on Snapchat or YouTube.

Your personas will also dictate what voice to adopt in your content. Brand messaging here could focus on Amelia's insecurity about her current path making a difference, and the small amount of time she could spend helping kids in her local community learn about good food. Brand messaging could also inform Amelia that volunteers with your organization have the opportunity to come on board as part- or full-time staff after a period of six months of service, so she knows her volunteering would also be useful in her search for a more fulfilling career. Much of the messaging targeted towards Amelia should imitate language she sees in her everyday life: light and clever, but informed about serious issues, and overall authentic in intent.

Avoid persona mistakes

Adele Revella, the founder and president of The Buyer Persona Institute, writes about four common mistakes organizations make when creating personas:

1. Making stuff up about buyers

There will often be holes in the information that you can gather easily about your audience. Not everything can be revealed by analytics or talking with your sales team. Don't just fill in these holes with what you imagine might be true. You have to dig deeper.

"If content marketing is going to benefit from buyer persona development, you will need to uncover specific insights that are unknown to your competitors or anyone inside your company," writes Revella. "This information will be so valuable that you would never post it on your website. However, it will tell you, with scary accuracy, exactly what you need to do to deliver content that persuades buyers to choose you."

Talk to the people who engage with your organization. Ask them why they did so. Ask them why they didn't go with someone else who does something similar. Ask them what they thought at each step in the process of interacting with your organization. "Each in-depth conversation should take 20 or 30 minutes, but the time it will save you in planning, writing, and revising content for each persona will be immeasurable," writes Revella. She recommends having these conversations several times a month to keep your information – and thus your personas – current.

2. Getting sidetracked by trivia

When you gather a lot of information, it can be difficult to decide what is relevant. You want the information that you use to be actionable when you are creating content. If you are an organization that promotes the welfare of children, knowing your audiences' preferred shoe brand doesn't matter. Unless you're TOMS.

Revella says there are a few pieces of information that you should prioritize. What are the problems that your persona dedicates time, money or political capital to? What does success mean to your persona (this can be either a tangible or intangible metric). What barriers does your persona face to interacting with your organization? How will your persona evaluate your service or cause?

3. Developing too many buyer personas

Many people think they should create a new persona for each demographic group. Not so, according to Revella. You only need to create a new persona when a segment of your audience differs in a way that's related directly to your cause. For example, if there is one group of people who have time that they'd like to volunteer, while another group has money they can donate, they should be represented by two different personas because these differences markedly change how they interact with your organization. It doesn't matter how old these people are or what gender.

4. Conducting scripted Q&A interviews

"Using a telephone script or online survey to learn about your buyers won't reveal anything you don't already know – inevitably, your buyer's first answer to any question will be something obvious, high level, and not particularly useful," writes Revella. "The structure imposed by surveys and scripts leads to nice charts, but it fails to reveal the new insights that you need."

Instead have a real conversation and ask open-ended questions. Ask probing questions. Let the answers you get lead you places you didn't know you needed to go. Follow-up is everything.

Revella emphasizes the importance of really understanding your audiences' perspective. Before you can be persuasive, you need to be empathetic.

When you know who your audience is, you can create the right kind of messages that will resonate with them, wherever they are. Your content will land more frequently, and you'll find inspiration to create new and different kinds of content. These personas will also be critical in developing your customer journey or user journey map.

How do professional digital strategists make personas?
Caleb Sexton of Maga Design says that often the larger the organization the more disconnected it is from customers, users, or donors. Personas are a step you can take to make a closer connection.

"Personas provide a bridge to better understanding what they think and feel about our offerings beyond simply quantitative market research," says Sexton. "They can act as a vehicle for identifying latent and unaddressed needs as well as pain points they may be facing not only with our brand, but competitor brands in the market as well."

How does Maga Design create personas? "Our approach is pretty straightforward: we first ask what is the job-to-be-done and in what context is it to be accomplished in? This allows us to dive in and figure out the various pains and gains that can act as a driver for triggering the need," says Sexton. "With this in mind we can then dive deeper to better understand the make up of the persona group and layer that with both qualitative and quantitative research. In many instances, we don't simply just make personas, but rather use them to build a journey map or day-in-the-life."

In a *New Yorker* profile by Elizabeth Kolbert on Democratic Senator from New York, Chuck Schumer, the power of the persona was illustrated with a striking example from politics:

If Schumer has a political philosophy, he owes it to a Long Island couple named Joe and Eileen Bailey. The Baileys live in Massapequa, a town on the South Shore, across the bay from Jones Beach. Joe works for an insurance company; Eileen is an administrative assistant in a physician's office. The couple have three children, two of whom are grown. Economically, the Baileys are doing O.K., but they worry about rising property taxes and what the future holds for their kids. They're not strong partisans. They feel that politicians of both parties sometimes condescend to them, something they hate. The Baileys voted for Bill Clinton twice, then, in 2000, after much agonizing, pulled the lever for George W. Bush.

This past November, the Baileys split their votes. Joe went with Trump, Eileen with Hillary. As for their kids, one was not yet eighteen, one voted for Clinton, and the third sat out the election. A few weeks ago, Schumer informed me that Eileen was feeling more confident about her vote, "not that she ever liked Hillary that much." Joe, meanwhile, was having second thoughts.

"He's getting a little queasiness in his stomach," Schumer said. "It just seems like amateur hour, and Joe's not an amateur. He's very good at what he does. He was angry at the liberal way, but he didn't think Trump would be like this."

To Schumer, the Baileys represent the sort of voters that the Democratic Party too often neglects, and that it needs to reach in order to survive. They are his reality check, which would be less noteworthy were they real.

Schumer dreamed up the Baileys during his first campaign for the Senate, in 1998.

Case Study: Save DC's Kids

PERSONAS

To ensure their digital strategy resonates with the majority of their constituents, Save DC's Kids put together three personas based on the populations that usually donate to the organization.

Doris Williams

Doris is a 73-year old DC native. She lives in a row house in Georgetown and stays busy by serving on the board of two nonprofits (she's the secretary for the board of the Georgetown Historical Society as well as the treasurer on the board of her church, Rock Creek Episcopal). She recently started taking classes at the Apple store to learn how to use her new iPhone 6.

Doris first got involved with Save DC's kids because her neighbor (and fellow Georgetown Historical Society board member) invited her to the organization's signature fundraiser, Cocktails for Kids, last spring.

Doris reads *The Washington Post* and *The Georgetowner* as soon as both papers land on her doorstep. Between board meetings and church gatherings, Doris is involved in a book club (which is really a wine and sometimes book club, but don't tell Doris we know her secret).

From June to September, Doris and her husband enjoy the Nantucket summer in their second home located in Madaket. Their two sons (who both live in the Boston suburbs) come to visit the first week in August with their children. (Doris loves her role as grandma and spoils her five grandchildren during their summer vacation and during frequent visits to DC.) To keep up with all of her family's activities, Doris uses Facebook and text messaging regularly.

Doris is one of Save's very wealthy donors. Her net worth is more than $5 million.

Donna Jackson

Similar to Doris, Donna is also a DC native. She's a single 40-something and a Howard University educated attorney working at the Public Defender Service for the District of Columbia (PDS). On Sundays, you can find Donna singing in the choir at the Michigan Avenue Church. She owns her one bedroom condo located three blocks from the Ballston Metro in Northern Virginia.

Donna stays current through online news sources she can easily access on her iPhone while commuting, including *The Huffington Post* and *Daily Kos*. Donna also subscribes to these publications by email and is quite responsive to email marketing from nonprofits, including Save. She doesn't have too much time for social media, but when she does, she catches up with her friends and a handful of nonprofits on Instagram and Facebook. She also uses Twitter to follow some DC policy related topics.

When she's done with her 70+ hour work week, Donna can be found grabbing drinks at the Busboys and Poets in Hyattsville or on the kickball field. She's a longtime member of Stonewall Kickball, DC's GLBT kickball league.

Donna makes $110,000 a year. Her finances are stretched thin because she has a significant amount of student loan debt and a mortgage to pay off, but she always carves out money in her budget to support causes she cares about. In addition to donating to Save DC's Kids, Donna is also a proud monthly donor to Whitman-Walker Health.

David Stein

Enthusiastic "Bernie Bro" David is 24-years old. This Vermonter turned Washingtonian sells solar panels door-to-door. Although he was raised Jewish, he now identifies as an atheist. His dream come true internship at Greenpeace two summers ago first brought him south to DC where he now resides in an eight-person group house in Columbia Heights. (You can thank him for the house's new account with Compost Cab.)

David is an Internet news junkie, never missing a Prince of Petworth, POPville or DCist post. He can name all the WAMU and NPR hosts as well as their corresponding show names by time slot and his secret crush is Audie Cornish. He never leaves home without his Nina Totenbag.

On weekends, David can be found hiking in Rock Creek Park, volunteering at FreshFarm farmers' markets, or spending time with his girlfriend, Jessica. (The two met as counselors at camp Ramah.)

David's Android phone is packed with apps he uses on the regular, including Instagram (especially the Instagram Stories feature), SnapChat and WhatsApp for texting. You won't find Facebook on David's phone because "that's an app for moms." If you want to reach David, don't try email or phone or even standard text; WhatsApp is the only way to go.

David makes $60,000, which doesn't go far in DC. He packs his lunch daily and saves money by riding his bike wherever he goes. David gives time as opposed to money to causes he cares about.

DEVELOP AUDIENCE PERSONAS
PERSONA A

THEIR STORY

_____

_____

_____

THEIR IDEAL EXPERIENCE

_____

_____

_____

THEIR GOALS

-
-
-
-

THEIR RESERVATIONS

-
-
-
-

PROFILE

UNDERGRADUATE DEGREE: _____

CURRENT INDUSTRY: _____ JOB FUNCTION: _____

AGE/FAMILY: _____ REGION: _____

TECHNICAL ABILITIES/ INFORMATION SOURCES

-
-
-
-

ATTRIBUTES

-
-
-
-

DEVELOP AUDIENCE PERSONAS
PERSONA B

THEIR STORY

_____

_____

_____

THEIR IDEAL EXPERIENCE

_____

_____

_____

THEIR GOALS

-
-
-
-

THEIR RESERVATIONS

-
-
-
-

PROFILE

UNDERGRADUATE DEGREE: _____

CURRENT INDUSTRY: _____ JOB FUNCTION: _____

AGE/FAMILY: _____ REGION: _____

TECHNICAL ABILITIES/ INFORMATION SOURCES

-
-
-
-

ATTRIBUTES

-
-
-
-

DEVELOP AUDIENCE PERSONAS
PERSONA C

THEIR STORY

_____

_____

_____

THEIR IDEAL EXPERIENCE

_____

_____

_____

THEIR GOALS

- ▪
- ▪
- ▪
- ▪

THEIR RESERVATIONS

- ▪
- ▪
- ▪
- ▪

PROFILE

UNDERGRADUATE DEGREE: _____

CURRENT INDUSTRY: _____   JOB FUNCTION: _____

AGE/FAMILY: _____   REGION: _____

TECHNICAL ABILITIES/ INFORMATION SOURCES

- ▪
- ▪
- ▪
- ▪

ATTRIBUTES

- ▪
- ▪
- ▪
- ▪

DEVELOP AUDIENCE PERSONAS
PERSONA D

THEIR STORY

_____

_____

_____

THEIR IDEAL EXPERIENCE

_____

_____

_____

THEIR GOALS
-
-
-
-

THEIR RESERVATIONS
-
-
-
-

PROFILE

UNDERGRADUATE DEGREE: _____

CURRENT INDUSTRY: _____   JOB FUNCTION: _____

AGE/FAMILY: _____   REGION: _____

TECHNICAL ABILITIES/ INFORMATION SOURCES
-
-
-
-

ATTRIBUTES
-
-
-
-

REFERENCES

Feldman, B. (2017, January 16). The Content Marketer's Approach to Successful Social Selling and Sales Enablement. Retrieved from https://www.marketingprofs.com/articles/2017/31408/the-content-marketers-approach-to-successful-social-selling

King, M. (2014, January 29). Personas: The Art and Science of Understanding the Person Behind the Visit. Retrieved from https://moz.com/blog/personas-understanding-the-person-behind-the-visit

Kolbert, E. (2017, March 27). Can Chuck Schumer Check Donald Trump? Retrieved from https://www.newyorker.com/magazine/2017/03/27/can-chuck-schumer-check-donald-trump

Lee, K. (2017, January 16). Social Media Goals: 7 Essential Strategies to Set Social Media Goals. Retrieved from https://blog.bufferapp.com/goal-setting-strategies

Leibtag, A. (2014). *The Digital Crown: Winning at Content on the Web*. Waltham, MA: Morgan Kaufmann.

Revella, A. (2012, August 23). How to Avoid 4 Buyer Persona Mistakes. Retrieved from http://contentmarketinginstitute.com/2012/08/4-common-persona-mistakes-to-avoid/

Sexton, C. (2017, July 19). Phone interview

CHAPTER 5
DESIGN A JOURNEY MAP

You can invest a lot of resources into designing a beautiful website, but it's moot if the user's complex experience isn't taken into account. And this doesn't just apply to website interactions; the way a user interacts with your organization across all media is something you need to understand before you can create content that resonates. Before you can determine the end of a user's journey (hopefully a conversion), you have to understand every step of the journey. This is why we create user journey maps.

A journey map allows you to walk in your audience's shoes. It allows you to understand your own organization as an outsider.

Paul Boag writes in *Smashing Magazine,* "Data often fails to communicate the frustrations and experiences of customers. A story can do that, and one of the best storytelling tools in business is the customer journey map."

Adam Richardson of Frog Design writes, "A customer journey map is a very simple idea: a diagram that illustrates the steps your customer(s) go through in engaging with your company, whether it be a product, an online experience, retail experience, or a service, or any combination. The more touchpoints you have, the more complicated – but necessary – such a map becomes. Sometimes customer journey maps are 'cradle to grave,' looking at the entire arc of engagement."

Here's another way to think about it, according to branding and UX expert Naomi Niles: *What you prefer or what your designer prefers doesn't matter if it's not getting you conversions.* Every part of your organization's interface should serve a user's journey, not the whims and desires of people inside the company.

Micah Solomon, a customer service and experience consultant, writes, "The point of doing a customer journey map is to look at your company from a different perspective than internally-viewed perspectives such as organizational charts. A journey map shows what the customer goes through from 'entering' your company from different points to finally concluding their business. Just remember that a customer's experience is more than a sum of the touchpoints."

No two actual audience experiences of your organization will be exactly alike, so a journey map is necessarily an average that represents a typical audience member and is based on research on your audience, much of which you already did to create personas.

A journey map is useful in presentations (and beyond)

Creating a user journey map is a very helpful way to understand what makes a user convert and what causes a user to lose interest. In a series of steps, you'll be able to see how a user first comes to your organization, what she experiences in those initial discovery phases, what makes her stay and convert, and what makes her a loyal advocate after the conversion is over.

Why do you have to visually map it out? It's useful for presentations where you need to show key stakeholders in your organization why you need to invest in certain areas of the digital experience. It's a visual tool that can show both how users currently interact with your organization and ways they *could or should* interact with your organization.

If a project or campaign has lived in a vague space for awhile, journey maps can bring tangible logistics into play, especially as it relates to conversions. Showing the team and other stakeholders how the campaign will work with a user in each phase can clarify the overall vision.

Quick Example: If you're trying to launch a video series that encourages donations to your organization, you can demonstrate the effectiveness of this campaign through a user journey map. Show that the user is not accustomed to being told stories by nonprofits – that she expects a bald request for money instead of a story that shows the value of involvement in the organization. Show how, after being exposed to the video via a local YouTube influencer, she clicks over to the landing page, and is led through a series of fun, educational steps that cause her to be emotionally invested in donating. After she makes the donation, show how follow-up with the influencer and other videos can remind her of the value of her contribution, and encourage her to be an advocate for the cause via her own social media.

Another way user journey maps are useful is for a deeper understanding of user behavior and how it relates to content you create. If you are struggling for creative guidance on content, knowing what your user expects vs. what she wants – and when she wants it – can help guide the tone, channel, and timing of content. For example, if she is expecting a request for money that involves lots of statistics in text form, surprise and delight her with a video that tells a very personal story from the point of view of a person who is helped by your cause.

The more you know about your customer, the better you can appeal to her interests. Knowing what her journey is as she is introduced to your organization can only help when making decisions about content meant to keep her interested.

"Most of all," writes Paul Boag, "a customer journey map puts the user front and center in the organization's thinking. It shows how mobile, social media and the web have changed customer behavior. It demonstrates the need for the entire organization to adapt."

Good thing you created all those personas

In the previous chapter, we discussed the why's and how's of audience personas, and provided an example of an audience persona that provides key information. I recommend creating two to four personas for your audience, keeping in mind that each persona likely has a slightly different user journey. Crafting those personas is where the major amount of research takes place. But once you do it, you'll know valuable information: what drives your customer, what motivates her, what turns her off, and where she gets her information.

You can use information from your persona to answer questions like where she first becomes aware of your organization, what factors in her life will play into her decision to interact with it, what kind of interaction she expects and wants, and the reason she would return to your organization in the future.

Main considerations for journey maps

What can you include in a journey map? The basics: your unique audience member relationship lifecycle with your organization. Include their expectations for your organization at each step and how well you are meeting those expectations.

What else? McorpCX's CEO of customer experience, Michael Hinshaw says that "nice-to-haves" include: brand perceptions, individual touchpoints, operational performance metrics, moments-of-truth, customer pain points, improvement opportunities, and other customer-facing elements that can provide great insight into your customers' experience. "Journey maps can also include behind-the-scenes people, processes, systems, and brand data," Hinshaw writes. Your map will reflect four major phases of a user's engagement:

1. **Awareness**—Where and how the user first encounters your organization. Is it through a YouTube influencer? A Facebook ad? Through which channels does she come to your organization and why does she click over?

2. **Acquisition**—When the user visits your site or wherever your digital campaign lives, what kinds of actions does she take? What does she click on and what does it drive her to do? What steps does your organization require her to take before deciding to make a monetary or converting decision?

3. **Retention**—At what moment does the user decide to convert? What prompts it and what happens immediately after to nurture it? How long is this after her first point of awareness of your organization? How does she see the fruits of her donation?

4. **Loyalty**—After the conversion is complete, what interactions does she have with your organization that push her to share the experience with her friends, either in person or on social media? Does she receive emails and how regularly?

A more detailed user journey map takes into account negative interactions as well. What causes the user to click away? When is the user unhappy with an interaction and how do you prompt that user to come back? These negative pain points could be useful when presenting a journey map that your campaign improves upon.

Creating a journey map: step by step

The Interaction Design Foundation, an independent nonprofit initiative established in Denmark, suggests a seven-step process for creating a journey map.

1. Align the mapping process with your core organizational objectives. What are your goals for this mapping exercise? What organizational needs do you intend to meet?

2. Bring together both analytical research (like website analytics and tracking your social presence) and anecdotal research (what have your audience members told you, what has your sales team told you about your audience) about your audience and their experience of your organization. You've already done a lot of this work creating your personas. How do your

users currently interact with your organization? On what channels? In what order? Where do you lose their interest?

3. List "touchpoints" and channels. A touchpoint is any moment when there is an interaction between your organization and an audience member. Looking at your website is a touchpoint. Receiving an email from you is a touchpoint. A call to your staff is a touchpoint. Making a donation is a touchpoint. Attending your event is one, too.

4. Create an empathy map, which examines how the user feels during each interaction. "You want to concentrate on how the customer feels and thinks as well as what they will say, do, hear, etc. in any given situation," according to the Interaction Design Foundation.

5. Sketch the user journey. According to the Interaction Design Foundation, "You can build a nice timeline map that brings together the journey over the course of time. You could also turn the idea into a video or an audio clip or use a completely different style of diagram. The idea is simply to show the motion of a customer through touchpoints and channels across your time period and how they feel about each interaction on that journey."

6. Iterate and produce your sketches. Bring in a graphic designer to create the clearest visual representation that you can.

7. Distribute and utilize. "You need to get [your journey map] out there to people and explain why it's important. Then it needs to be put to use. You should be able to define KPIs around the ideal journey, for example, and then measure future success as you improve the journey," according to the Interaction Design Foundation.

Creating your journey map should allow you to take action. Michael Hinshaw writes, "It should identify a few quick fixes, including opportunities to boost enjoyment and improve the journey… In brief, mapping the journey should help lead to specific actions – actions that improve the experience and drive the ROI to justify the effort and increase internal support."

With each step of your journey map that you write – with your user personas handy – make sure to consider these lenses:

*   **Context**—Does this step make sense in the context of your user? Look at your user persona. Does the step you are expecting your user to make fit into the context of her life? Is there a way you could make the step a better fit?

- **Progression**—Does this step naturally arise from the step before it? Does it prompt the user to take the next step?

- **Devices**—On what device is your user interacting with your organization at this step? Is it a different device from other steps, and should your content be different because of that? How does the medium affect the likelihood of taking the next step?

- **Functionality**—Does your interface encourage the kinds of actions you're expecting the user to take? On a more technical level, what about your UX could be improved upon, or what about it already makes this step seamless for the user?

- **Emotion**—Think empathically here. What is your user feeling at the moment of this step? Is she frustrated? Does she not want to be sold to? Does she want more storytelling? A clearer vision of what a commitment looks like? Really put yourself in the user's shoes to understand how emotion drives decisions.

It's important to remember that journey maps come in all shapes and sizes. There's no right or wrong way to design a journey map as long as it includes the main elements and makes visual sense to the stakeholders and professionals using the tool.

Michael Hinshaw warns that creating a journey map could cause "analysis paralysis." Deep research into your audience will produce a lot of data and it can be tempting to try to include a lot of it in your journey map. "Don't," emphasizes Hinshaw. "Remember that [the journey map is] a tool to help you easily understand customers and their needs. That core message can get lost in the details."

To test the veracity of your journey map, you may want to have someone "mystery shop" your organization. This means asking an objective third party to go through the many touchpoints that audience members have with your organization and report back on their experience. Does your e-newsletter provide the inspiration that you hope it does? Does calling your organization with a question result in the information needed? A mystery shopper can find out for sure.

Case Study: Save DC's Kids

JOURNEY MAP

Save DC's Kids' Journey Map for Doris:
Doris first learned about Save DC's Kids through a neighbor who invited her to the organization's signature event, Cocktails for Kids. By RSVPing through the event's online registration form, Doris's email address was captured and added to the organization's CRM,

Salesforce. Once Doris's name and email address were logged in Save's Salesforce instance, an automatic wealth screen was triggered, flagging the fact that she has made several large donations to other organizations in the recent past.

Once put in the exclusive major donor category, Doris is treated to one-on-one meetings with Save development staff and opted out of low dollar email asks as well. She is added to Save's elite group of high dollar donors, the Impact Donor Circle, a community of people who are able to make gifts of $1,000 or more. The Impact Donor Circle members receive invites to exclusive events and are able to sit in on special, strategic planning conference calls hosted by the Save Executive Director as well.

Save DC's Kids' Journey Map for Donna:
Donna's path to Save involvement began on Facebook. She saw a post about enrollment in before and after-care that a friend had liked and decided to like the organization's page herself. Donna had never heard of Save DC's Kids before, but after reading a bit more about them she knew they were filling a service gap she had seen many times during her work as a public defender.

After becoming a Facebook fan, Save's end of year donation match video popped up in Donna's feed. She watched the short video while commuting to work and was so moved she decided to make her first gift to the organization. It was being triple matched by a major donor and Donna was attracted to the concept of stretching one dollar into four for such a worthy cause. When completing the mobile donation form on her phone, Donna was asked which area of Save's program focus she was most interested in supporting and she chose nutritional meals and snacks.

Once that first donation was made, an interest area flag was created on Donna's record in Salesforce and she has been tracked to become a Save Star. The organization's drip email campaign has kicked off with a welcome from Save's executive director. Donna then began getting direct mail from Save specifically about the organization's work on nutritional meals, including the most recent mailing that includes a recipe card and healthy snack ideas compiled by local chefs just for Save DC's Kids afterschool snack program.

As of this month, Donna is considered fully cultivated as a donor; she is getting regular email, social media, and direct mail contact all about Save's healthy meals and snacks program. Next up, Save will work to turn Donna into a monthly donor.

Save DC's Kids' Journey Map for David:

Remember that David can give of his time, but not support Save financially. He connected with a member of the Save Star program, Erica, while selling solar panels (those Petworth residents are so friendly). Erica was interested in a solar panel quote and mentioned her volunteer work with Save during her meeting with David. Erica then invited David to join her for a teacher training committee meeting, asked for his email address, and followed up with an email invite to the gathering. At the same time, Erica also shared David's email with the Save Star coordinator on staff and his information was entered into Save's CRM system.

David began getting emails from Save specifically targeting possible volunteer opportunities. David was successfully wooed and became a Save volunteer. David is not asked for money regularly, but twice a year all Save volunteers receive a soft fundraising ask from a fellow volunteer. The end of year ask in 2017 was a $10 request from volunteers, plus a challenge to raise 10 more dollars from nine friends, for a total of $100. David accepted the challenge and raised the money in less than a week through a personal GoFundMe page and some plugs on his personal Instagram feed. (Turns out, photos David took of teachers who are super passionate about their work getting trained on how to be better teachers were pretty compelling to David's friends.)

CREATE A JOURNEY MAP

PLATFORM OR MEDIUM	AWARENESS	CONSIDERATION	ACTION	RETENTION	ADVOCACY

REFERENCES

Boag, P. (2015, January 16). All You Need To Know About Customer Journey Mapping. Retrieved from https://www.smashingmagazine.com/2015/01/all-about-customer-journey-mapping/

Hinshaw, M. (2012, October 30). Customer Journey Mapping: 10 Tips For Beginners. Retrieved from http://www.cmo.com/opinion/articles/2012/10/30/customer-journey-mapping-10-tips-for-beginners.html

Interaction Design Foundation. (2017, November). Customer Journey Maps - Walking a Mile in Your Customer's Shoes. Retrieved from https://www.interaction-design.org/literature/article/customer-journey-maps-walking-a-mile-in-your-customer-s-shoes

Richardson, A. (2010, November 15). Using Customer Journey Maps to Improve Customer Experience. Retrieved from https://hbr.org/2010/11/using-customer-journey-maps-to

Solomon, M. (2016, May 09). Transform Your Customer Service And Customer Experience In 12 Steps. Retrieved from https://www.forbes.com/sites/micahsolomon/2016/05/09/12-action-steps-that-will-transform-your-customer-service-and-customer-experience/#38456ee86a8b

CHAPTER 6
IDENTIFY KEY CHANNELS

First, you don't have to be on all channels

You need to be on the channels where your audience hangs out. But that could mean a few different things depending on your organization. It could mean that you need to be on every major channel in some way, big or small. It could mean that the content you create for Facebook is vastly different from the content you create for email blasts. It could mean that you are on different channels at different points in the sales cycle or for different kinds of digital campaigns.

Here's what it *doesn't* mean:

- You need to be on every channel equally.
- You only need to be on _____ channel because it's the only one that matters.

- You need to be on _____ channel because it's the hot new mobile app.

There isn't an easy mathematical solution to deciding which channels to create content for. Knowing where your organization and content need to be requires more than just knowing what channels are popular right now. It requires a deep investigation into the kinds of interactions your organization wants, a thorough understanding of who your audience is (those personas you made) and insights into how and why they make decisions (those journey maps you made).

Know your channels – The three M's

One useful way to evaluate a digital channel is to look at it through the lens of the three M's: is it meaningful to your audience? Is it manageable for your team? And is what happens there measurable for your campaign?

- **Meaningful**: Is the channel you've selected meaningful to your audience? Is the content you'll create for that channel meaningful? Identify the channel's strengths and major audience segments, and determine if those align with your organization. If they don't align, your presence and content there will ring false, both internally and with your target audience.

- **Manageable**: Are you already juggling too many channels for the amount of staff you have? It's a very bad marketing move to announce your presence on a new channel and then disappear because you don't have a team to manage it. When evaluating whether or not a channel is appropriate for you, investigate whether you would need to create entirely new content for it and if you can handle that, or if you already have content that is adaptable to the channel.

- **Measurable**: Is the value of that channel measurable? This might be the hardest thing to determine. Some channels, like Twitter, have proprietary analytics features. Some you can measure via other reporting platforms. But others might have value that isn't immediately measurable. Are you willing to forgo measurement to be on the channel? Perhaps. But it takes some consideration to make that decision.

Types of channels

Gini Dietrich's PESO model is the most current and useful way to understand the kinds of channels available to you. It divides channels into four main sectors: paid, earned, shared, and owned. This taxonomy can be helpful when you're looking at where you've been and where to go next. You might find your organization heavy in paid and shared channels, but lacking in leveraging the owned and earned channels. You also might find some areas of overlap, where you can maximize the reach of your content because it's useful across channels.

Here's a breakdown of the kinds of channels:

- **Paid**: These channels include paid ads on Facebook and Twitter, any kind of lead generation your team is doing, and sponsored content. In more traditional marketing, this segment would include print ads or commercials.

- **Earned**: This is publicity for your organization that you don't pay for, meaning press releases you send that get written up on other sites, mentions by bloggers or other influencers, and basically anywhere you get your name in print. Think old school journalism and PR via digital channels.

- **Shared**: Shared media includes social media channels where you grow a following. Many organizations already use this as a main source of communications, but it's useful to look at how much you're leveraging it. Are your organization's major moves always posted across your social channels? Does your following engage with your posts on social channels?

- **Owned**: Owned media usually lives on your website or blog, and includes any content you create yourself – blog posts, original videos, infographics, research write-ups, case studies, etc. As content marketing (using your original owned media to engage an audience) grows, an investment in your owned media is important.

Don't get confused if your strategy lives in the overlaps of these segments. A brand story video that you pay to promote on Facebook exists in the overlap of paid and owned. A relationship with a digital influencer who tells their audience about your organization is part shared and part earned.

Let personas dictate channels and let channels dictate content

A thorough knowledge of your audience personas will reveal which channels you need to be on. A millennial audience member who is looking to switch careers and wants a volunteer-to-part-time gig will probably be looking more at LinkedIn and Facebook for those opportunities, and probably not Twitter or your blog.

Knowing which channels to focus your campaign on can be helpful in knowing what content to create. Content creation doesn't happen in a vacuum. Perhaps the most important thing about channel knowledge is the *guidance it provides for your content*. Once you've decided on channels that are appropriate for your personas, you can use all of that information (the persona preferences and the kind of content that does well on that channel) to write the perfect blog post, create the most engaging video, or craft the most shareable tweets.

Multichannel campaigns

Way back in 2005, *AdWeek* reported Gap's plans for a multi-channel marketing campaign referred to as "Find Your Favorite Fit." The campaign suggested that a pair of jeans should suit a person's tastes as uniquely as a favorite song. Gap partnered with iTunes, which was relatively new at the time, to offer potential customers a free download in exchange for trying on a new style. Along with print advertisements in a number of popular magazines, the campaign included TV ads featuring musicians including Jason Mraz, Joss Stone, Alanis Morisette, and John Legend, who all recorded songs for a CD that Gap sold in stores.

It was an ambitious multi-channel campaign suited to its time. And yet Gap wasn't done experimenting with its tone or with how it represented itself to potential customers. The same year, the company produced a TV ad that announced the store's plans to reconfigure the layout of its stores. Although that ad, directed by filmmaker Spike Jonze, had a relatively short run in 2005, it has since enjoyed a greater legacy online.

Every channel has a unique audience. In a comprehensive report on multichannel digital marketing, Digital Doughnut and Episerver found that nearly every marketer "agree[s] that a multi-channel strategy that allows them to target customers is important for their organization." The same report found that fewer than half of surveyed businesses don't think they have the skills to use multiple channels effectively, and fewer than one-third feel "highly confident" that they can meet the goals of their own multi-channel campaigns.

"With a multi-channel strategy, you can be where your targeted customers are – whatever channel, platform, or device they may be using at that particular time," write CJG Digital Marketing.

Which is just another way of saying what Gap said a decade ago: *fit matters.* With every new channel you add to your digital marketing campaign, you need to know how to fit your message to your audience. Let's take a look at three of the most popular marketing channels (as of 2017) and offer a few tips to help you fit your message to the audience on the other end. Keep in mind that there are many channels out there and you should use your personas and journey map to understand the channels and platforms you should be focusing on.

In the stream

Your audience on Twitter – one of every four people online, typically college-educated and almost certainly between the ages of 16 and 50 – is in the stream with you. "Because Twitter is an open, real-time network, you can tap into the behaviors, demographics, interests and more of your audience," writes Lauren Dugan for *AdWeek.*

Therefore, to use Twitter effectively you need to keep up with your intended audience. Let's get literal: if the stream is *actually a stream*, and everyone in your audience is linking hands to float down the river together, you want to join them.

Companies depend on their own relevance, and Twitter is the ultimate proving ground. As your audience shares in real-time, seek out those demographic cues – those hashtags and keywords – that will grant you access to their circle. That way, you can target your audience with precision.

Or, invite people to *your* circle. "Your audience probably has multiple touchpoints with your brand, in addition to Twitter," says Dugan. "So if you are running a contest of any type, promote it across all of your marketing channels – social media as well as your blog, website and wherever else it makes sense. This will ensure that your audience sees the contest wherever they are online." The same goes for live events, where Dugan suggests using Twitter the same way that many people do when they live-tweet their favorite TV shows. Offer a second glimpse at your organization in real-time.

In the flow

Audience demographics on YouTube are more evenly distributed; for instance, your average YouTube viewer is more likely to be in the 45-54 age range than eighteen to twenty-four. And it pays to know niche demographics: Digiday has a few handy charts that underscore huge differences in audience gender for a number of eclectic subjects, from "soccer" to "East Asian music" to "beauty and style."

As with Twitter – or with any channel – knowing where your goals dovetail with your audience's interests is essential. What is specific to each channel in your digital campaign is *how you appeal* to those interests. And YouTube's audience is perhaps the most particular about how they receive advertisements.

YouTube itself refers to video's "emotional power." Real emotional power requires an audience's engagement. YouTube is designed to enable marketers to make good on an audience's investment. Organizations that use TrueView ads can attract only those audience members with an authentic interest (YouTube says "all of the top 100 global brands" have done just that) and use AdWords to remarket videos to a growing, engaged audience.

Once your audience has shown their investment – once they've jumped into the flow of your video – then you can adjust the flow accordingly and sustain your emotional power. Remember Old Spice's "The Man Your Man Could Smell Like" ad? Here's how Wieden + Kennedy followed it:

> *Shortly after the debut of this spot, W+K developed an interactive digital campaign capitalising on the popularity of the "Old Spice Guy." The result was the Old Spice Response*

Campaign – an experiment in real-time branding featuring the Old Spice Guy posting personal video responses to fans online.

In the end, 186 personal video messages responding to fans' comments on social sites Facebook, Twitter and others were scripted, filmed and then posted online in just over two and a half days of production, with many of the videos churned out from start to finish in just 10 to 15 minutes. The work went on to record more than 65 million views, making it one of the fastest-growing and most popular online interactive advertising campaigns in history.

In the company of friends

Facebook users connect with friends across generations and along neighborhood lines; the channel offers an increasingly accurate window into a version of each user's real-world social networks.

Accordingly, Facebook users want to trust others, and want their social network to be as personalized and as orderly as their own lives, if not more so. On Facebook, be personal, be organized, and be studious.

"Being recognizable is important to getting found and Liked," writes Ginny Mineo, manager of content marketing strategy at HubSpot's Marketing Blog. Facebook users want to identify you – by your picture and your "About" section and your pinned post. Once an audience recognizes you, then they want to feel *recognized by you*. The channel, writes Mineo, "has a number of targeting tools that enable you to segment your organic posts by age, gender, education, etc." But don't overdo the posts, and don't forget to use multimedia; if you do, then your audience will think of you as the boring chatterbox at the next neighborhood party.

As for being studious, Mineo says that tracking URLs and Facebook insights should provide you with plenty of data about how and when people respond favorably to your posts. After all, good friends pay attention.

Find channels that provide authenticity

According to AdEspresso, social media platforms like Snapchat feel authentic. "Social media sites in general are great for rapport building, and in some cases, giving the 'behind the scenes' look to users. Snapchat amplifies this facet of social media marketing; it's more about what's happening right now." Communicating via Snapchat has immediacy; it doesn't feel like you've been planning your video for months (even if you have) instead it seems dashed off, but in a good way.

Also with Snapchat, you can reach a new audience. Want to reach a younger audience? Snapchat could be your way in. "CNN, for example, connected with more Millenials on Snapchat than they had through their site; it was an audience they'd previously had some trouble connecting with," according to AdEspresso.

Consider your available resources
Different channels require different skills and content types.

For example:

- **Images.** You can share images on Snapchat or Instagram that were taken with your camera phone and edited or uploaded from your saved photos. Snaps are best in a portrait format, which is the only way to view them. Facebook is also a largely visual platform.
- **Videos.** Videos can be shared on Snapchat, as long as they're kept under 10 seconds long (though some crafty users have apparently figured out hacks around that). They can be edited like images. Longer videos can be shared on Facebook or used in a campaign on YouTube, for example.
- **Text**: Short and snappy text belongs on Twitter and Facebook. If it's funny, even better. Longer, more complex text belongs on your website in the form of a blog, which can be sent out as a press release or you can publish it on LinkedIn.

Need a little inspiration?
If you've been mostly using text to communicate, transitioning to photographs can be intimidating. Winnie Lui, storyteller and author at

CauseVox has some tips for successful Instagram images for nonprofit organizations. She suggests:

- Human centric images that connect to viewers' hearts. World Bicycle Relief uses images of smiling Malawian students who you can donate bikes to. Lui points out that photographs of the people you are helping are always very effective. It shows impact. Including several people in your images can show a larger scale of impact than showing just one person. (Although showing just one person can also be good. It feels very personal.)

- Demonstrate the urgent need that your work addresses. A NeverThirst Instagram post shows two drinking glasses full of water. The water in one is yellow and murky because it hasn't been filtered. The second shows clear, filtered water. The organization's impact is made clear (please excuse the pun) without saying a word.

- If you have a celebrity involved with your organization, show him or her in your images. People respond to people they recognize. Roots and Shoots posts images of famous environmentalist Jane Goodall on Instagram.

- People like beautiful images. Earth Rights uses filters and great lighting in their Instagram images. The images get shared because they are pleasing.

- The best images tell a story. The 'To Write Love On Her Arms' Instagram account shows images of people adding slips of paper on which they have written their burdens and their hopes to a wall of similar slips of paper.

Case Study: Save DC's Kids

KEY CHANNELS

Save DC's Kids focuses on four main online channels to communicate with their audiences:

Website

This is the channel with the fewest number of eyeballs on it. Save treats their website as a virtual "lobby" for their organization in which different audiences gather and then find the metaphorical "room" they're looking for based on different interest areas or needs. The website features images of children that have been helped by Save's programs (once mom or dad sign a release, that is). The site does include a few photos of teachers, but testing showed that photos of kids yielded more clicks. The website tone is somewhat serious and on the more formal side since it needs to have broader appeal. Save didn't have a mobile friendly site for years, but after two Save Stars insisted on this in 2016, the organization made the investment in updating their site and it is now responsive.

Words to describe the Save website tone: thorough, accessible, credible.

Email

Save DC's Kids uses VerticalResponse, an email marketing tool that integrates well with their Salesforce CRM. The organization's email marketing efforts are segmented by interest area.

1. Emails going to the segment of the Save community that has expressed interest in nutrition tend to have a bit more data in them to illustrate the science behind healthy meals and snacks. From time to time, they feature recipe and meal planning tips, too.

2. The before and after-care segment can be characterized by a heart-to-heart connection and usually includes stories of kids directly served by Save. The tone is much more emotional and less data driven.

3. Save's emails about the teacher training program are a happy combination of the heartfelt approach and the data driven approach. They, too, include stories of kids that Save has helped along with quotes from parents and community members.

Facebook

Save has done extensive testing on Facebook. The data shows that images of kids Save has worked with perform best when coupled with quotes from parents. Statistics do not resonate with the Save population on Facebook, so the organization has chosen a much more story-centric approach on this channel and steers clear of too many numbers or facts. They have also seen a huge jump in response rate when storytelling videos are incorporated, further reinforcing the storytelling and emotionally connected tone. Lastly, Save DC's Kids had fun (and saw the number of comments and shares increase) when they hosted a "Facebook takeover" by a local DC celebrity. Chef Carla Hall has participated in the healthy meals program run by Save and her Facebook takeover was by far the most successful with over 800 likes, shares, and comments in 24 hours.

Words to describe the Save Facebook tone: warm, inviting, dynamic.

Instagram

Of all four of Save's different channels, Facebook is the least formal. Returning to the personas associated with Save's work, Instagram is used by folks like David and less by folks like Doris. The organization uses Instagram "traditions" such as #TBT or #WCW in addition to pop turns of phrase ("all the feels") which are popular with the younger segment of their audience.

Words to describe the Save Instagram tone: fresh, fun, current.

IDENTIFY KEY CHANNELS

OTHERS:

OTHERS:

OTHERS:

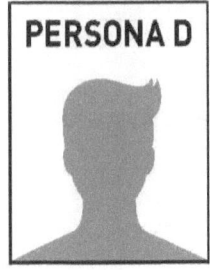

OTHERS:

REFERENCES

Blattberg, E. (2015, April 24). The demographics of YouTube, in 5 charts. Retrieved from https://digiday.com/media/demographics-youtube-5-charts/

Dugan, L. (2015, October 10). 5 Ways to Integrate Twitter Into Your Cross-Channel Marketing Campaigns. Retrieved from http://www.adweek.com/digital/5-ways-to-integrate-twitter-into-your-cross-channel-marketing-campaigns/#/

Gotter, A. (2017, March 29). The Ultimate Guide to Snapchat Marketing. Retrieved from https://adespresso.com/blog/ultimate-guide-marketing-snapchat/

Gregorio, J. (2016, May 23). 8 Benefits of Multi-Channel Digital Marketing [Infographic]. Retrieved from https://www.business2community.com/infographics/8-benefits-multi-channel-digital-marketing-infographic-01551178#s5Yjm7G9bMjL0mrL.97

Iliff, R. (2014, December 05). Why PR is embracing the PESO model. Retrieved from http://mashable.com/2014/12/05/public-relations-industry/#kSm.TlIHNOqr

Lui, W. (2016, August 16). 6 Nonprofits On Instagram Who Are Getting It Right. Retrieved from https://www.causevox.com/blog/best-nonprofits-instagram/

Mineo, G. (2017, September 19). The Do's and Don'ts of How to Use Facebook for Business [Infographic]. Retrieved from https://blog.hubspot.com/marketing/dos-donts-facebook-business-infographic#sm.001mv7tbfpyxefc113g1q7zznsh8j

Watt, N. (2015, March). 2015 Multichannel Digital Marketing Report. Retrieved from http://www.episerver.com/globalassets/assets-website-structure/New-Folder9/research--reports/dd-episerver-multichannel-new-branding.pdf

Wieden Kennedy Portland. (2011). Case Study: Old Spice Response Campaign. Retrieved from http://www.dandad.org/en/d-ad-old-spice-case-study-digital-marketing/

YouTube. (2017). YouTube for Press. Retrieved from https://www.youtube.com/yt/about/press/

CHAPTER 7
DEVELOP A CONTENT STRATEGY

You've defined your goals. You know your audience. You've identified the right channels. Now, what are you going to say? More importantly, what is the conversation you want to have?

Marketing guru Doug Kessler says, "Traditional marketing talks at people. Content marketing talks with them." I like this quote because it hits on one of the biggest paradigm shifts in contemporary marketing from one-way communication to two-way interaction.

Digital audiences no longer want to listen to traditional advertising efforts and they no longer have to. Instead, they can easily engage with content from brands across devices, across channels, and across their days. For an organization to be relevant and necessary, content needs to fall seamlessly into the rhythm of its audience's lives. It should be useful.

We live squarely in the age of content marketing, and we're lucky we do. The core of your marketing strategy is the content you create and curate. It's what attracts and compels your target audience. It represents your organization's beliefs and resonates with the beliefs of your customers. The connection made via good content is what marketers do it all for.

Creating quality, compelling content, however, is hard. All the digital strategy steps we've discussed in previous chapters – honing your purpose, setting marketing goals, understanding your audience through personas, and targeting specific channels on which to reach them – is essential to creating good content. Once you know what you believe, what your audience believes, and where they're hanging out, you're ready to deploy your content.

I like to use the "Three C's" mnemonic as a barometer to gauge the potential success of my content. Any piece of content you create – a whitepaper, a short video, a podcast episode – should meet these criteria: is it consistent? Is it customized? And is it constructive?

Three C's

Is the content consistent?

One of the biggest rookie mistakes when it comes to content marketing is ignoring consistency in your content creation. If you're on several channels at once, there's a tendency to create content for each channel that has messages that aren't in line with content on the other channels – or your own organization's beliefs, for that matter.

If you've already spent time zeroing in on your brand promise, you should then extrapolate from that core promise to articulate a couple key messages you want to be associated with. Any more than three or four messages will likely confuse your audience, so start small. But try more than one, as you might need a variety to resonate with different kinds of audiences.

For example, your brand promise for your nonprofit might be something like, "We believe that everyone should have access to clean water, and our goal is to bring education and resources to small villages in West Africa so that their water supply systems may be healthy and sustainable." One of the messages you might want to be associated with could be, "Water education leads to innovation and freedom." Therefore, when you're thinking about kinds of tweets that curate content from other sources, you're going to want to look for innovative infrastructure examples from across the world. When you're thinking about short videos to create, you might show a clip of a water system you've helped build in use in a village. When you're considering guests for your podcast episode, you'll want to look for innovation experts who can discuss long-term effects of access to clean water.

What you shouldn't do is convey a message of lighthearted humor on Twitter and then use shocking photos on Instagram. Not only are those messages not consistent with each other, but they aren't consistent with your brand promise, either.

Aha Media Group's methodology involving content values is useful when crafting the messages you want to convey with your content. Ahava Leibtag explains that content values are "not branding or identity pillars, and they aren't voice and tone. Instead, content values should encompass how you make decisions about what, how, when and to whom you publish." At Aha Media Group, they value content that is straightforward, valuable for their target audiences, never jargon heavy, and conversational, but not too informal. They value accessibility and it shows in every piece of content they create.

Is it customized?

Know thy channel. Customize your content for the specific channel, or risk looking like an amateur. The previous chapter covers how to identify which channels are best for you, and once you've discovered your channel mix sweet spot, you can start tailoring content for each channel. The key word here is "tailor." Don't create a piece of content and then expect it to be easily distributed across channels without customization. Audiences expect different kinds of content on different channels, and if yours doesn't fit in with (or innovate within) the channel standard, your content will be overlooked.

For example, if your clean water nonprofit creates a whitepaper – which is a good idea, as it provides a lot of useful content for immediate use – you should then look at how you can break out parts of that whitepaper for different channels. Perhaps the part of the whitepaper that explains the nuts and bolts of the organization's efforts can be turned into an engaging how-to blog post. Perhaps the parts that discuss results can be turned into an infographic that would be good for sharing on Facebook.

What you definitely shouldn't do is use parts of the whitepaper word-for-word across channels. What the classic whitepaper audience expects and likes is not necessarily what the classic Facebook audience expects and likes. Understanding what kinds of audiences hang out on which channels will help guide how to tailor existing content for specific channels.

Is it constructive?

Remember: good content marketing talks *with* your audience. Talking with them means not only talking about what they're already discussing, but answering a question they're asking, addressing a pain point they don't know how to solve. Any good piece of content is good because it's useful and constructive for the target audience. Its use could come in many forms. It could be funny, poignant, or hip. It could contain knowledge about how to do something. It could contain results and statistics in the form of a case study. It could be a conversation-starter, fostering community and discussion. It could simply be entertaining. But whatever the content is, its constructive use should be clear to you before you distribute it across channels.

If your clean water nonprofit wants to create content that has a clear use, make sure to add a call to action somewhere in it, i.e. where your audience can sign up to advocate or donate. If your constructive use is educational, make sure to promote your content with snackable bits of information, statistics, or facts that your audience will remember. Along those same lines, make your educational or informational content shareable. If something is shareable, it is useful. People like to share content that their friends find interesting. If you create something that looks nice, has a catchy headline, and clear takeaways, its "shareability" goes through the roof.

What you shouldn't do is create content with no clear goal in mind. What is your content going to do? Why will your audience click on it? Why will they continue to read it? What part of it will make them share it? If you can't answer all of these questions before distributing your content, it's likely not going to be useful for your audience.

The challenge and the thrill of content creation

We're in the midst of a content arms race right now – those with the most engaging, compelling, and useful content always win. In one way, it's made digital marketing more cutthroat. When everyone has a voice, the voice standards are raised. In another way, it has made marketing more fun and exciting than ever before. When you get to create content that truly communicates your brand beliefs and brand promise, real connection is possible. You're no longer bound by traditional marketing and advertising formats. You have permission to think outside the box in an effort to get inside your target community. Consider the content part of your digital strategy to be the part where the art of marketing is really on display.

How to start from the beginning on social platforms

Nothing is less professional than a half-completed profile. Choose great photos. Invest in them. Good imagery is half the battle.

Put together a great bio. Think about your unique value proposition and how you set yourself apart. According to Inbound Rocket:

> Accurately explain who you are and what your company does. Personify your brand. A lot of social networks are more lighthearted than their official company website counterparts. Don't worry too much about writing a formal biography; this

is the place to show off the fun side of your brand. Try using specific words that your ideal customer would use to describe themselves. Although keywords on most social networks are not directly searchable, viewers will immediately know that you are a relevant account for them to follow or like.

Twitter

With Twitter, you'll need to build a following of people who need the information that you have to offer. This will take time.

1) Follow people that might want to follow you. You can find these people in a few different ways. They might be following organizations like yours on Twitter. They might be tweeting things related to the problems that your organization addresses or asking questions about those topics. You can answer their questions. You can start conversations. You can follow them and hope that they follow you back.

2) Enter conversations that are already happening on Twitter about issues that you have great content for and link back to your great content.

3) Be a place on Twitter where people who share your concerns can also get information. You can certainly link to your own content, but also provide links to other interesting content that you find.

4) Have buttons on your site that make it easy for people to follow you on Twitter. In addition, provide buttons on your site that make it easy for people to share your content on Twitter.

Facebook

Facebook is more of a broadcast platform than Twitter. I would suggest putting up little teasers for pages from your site with quality pictures on a regular schedule. Have buttons on your site that make it easy for people to share your content on Facebook. Make it easy to follow you on Facebook. Eventually, you might want to invest in small amounts in paid advertising on Facebook.

LinkedIn

You can publish articles directly on LinkedIn that will be shared with people you are connected to. They are also visible to people you don't know if they search the keywords that you mark your content with. Publishing teaser articles with links to the full article can be a way of reaching your key population.

Beyond social platforms

Be your own PR person. Brainstorm about what kind of websites or even print publications might be a good fit for articles written by you or places that might be responsive to a press release. Reach out to publications that already serve the audience that you want to reach. Give them guest posts that link back to your site or your social profiles. Offer to do an interview about your area of expertise.

There are major online publishers, such as *Forbes* or *The Huffington Post* (amongst others), where you could submit an article about your ideas and expertise. If your organization has a wide online presence, it will feed back into your social media presence.

Case Study: Save DC's Kids

CONTENT STRATEGY

In order to implement a successful campaign, Save DC's Kids' staff is preparing several different types of content:

Facebook, Email and Instagram

- Images of kids that Save has worked with, images of teachers Save has trained, and images of volunteers.
- Healthy snack preparation ideas as well as images of Save volunteers prepping meals and snacks for kids.
- Facebook or Instagram takeover content or guest-curated email (written by notable DC residents including Chefs Carla Hall and Jose Andres as well as the mayor and then posted as Save with credit to the original author).
- A small number of infographic posts with statistics about the importance of healthy food for kids and other numbers showcasing Save's impact.

- Links to articles from local and national publications that mention Save and the impact the organization is making in DC.

- Information about donation matches (similar to the one that prompted Donna to get involved with Save in the first place).

- Behind the scenes preparations as well as RSVP information for Save events such as Cocktails for Kids.

- Save Star recruitment content including images of existing volunteers and volunteers interacting with kids.

- Facebook Live and Instagram Story opportunities (which cannot be recorded in advance) of special events and everyday volunteer opportunities as well as Save Star appreciation ceremonies.

- Short video interviews with families who have been helped by Save's services as well as posts with quotes from the interviews.

Daily Facebook Posts

A core component of the Save strategy will take place on Facebook (you may recall that two out of the three personas described in the Audience chapter use Facebook regularly). To this end, Save is preparing at least one post daily for Facebook. Save plans to increase the number of eyes on their Facebook feed by specifically posting photographs from events and volunteer opportunities and tagging the images so they show up in the personal feeds of Save Stars and other supporters.

Daily Instagram Posts

Since Instagram is a high volume channel, Save is preparing one post per day for their Instagram feed and, at times, two. They're also planning to use Instagram Stories as a way to cover larger events and fundraisers. Save will also use a contest feature asking followers to post their favorite healthy after-school snack and tag the organization to be entered to win a free meal at Jaleo. This will not only build awareness of the importance of healthy snacking but also increase Save's Instagram following.

Email Marketing Content

Save's email marketing content is divided into three segments corresponding to the three different program areas the organization works on. The staff will prepare three emails for each of the three topic areas (nine emails total). Each campaign will include:

1. Resources (such as recipes for after-school snacks or stats on after-care importance)
2. Action opportunities (join us for Cocktails for Kids, volunteer to help out with teacher training, become a Save Star, share content on social media)
3. Donation ask (just $50 provides lunches and snacks for one student for an entire week or donation match)

DEVELOP A CONTENT STRATEGY

PERSONA _____

USER STATE _____

JOURNEY (INCLUDING TASKS)	CHANNELS	CONTENT

PERSONA _____

USER STATE _____

JOURNEY (INCLUDING TASKS)	CHANNELS	CONTENT

REFERENCES

Kessler, D. (2017, April 25). The Content Assembly Line is Broken. Retrieved from http://contentmarketinginstitute.com/author/doug-kessler/

Leibtag, A. (2016, March 15). What Type of Content Values Should You Have? Retrieved from https://ahamediagroup.com/blog/2016/03/what-type-of-content-values-should-you-have/

Nielsen Norman Group. (n.d.). Jakob Nielsen, Ph.D. and Principal at Nielsen Norman Group. Retrieved June 30, 2017, from https://www.nngroup.com/people/jakob-nielsen/

Nielson, J. (2008, May 06). How Little Do Users Read? Retrieved from https://www.nngroup.com/articles/how-little-do-users-read/

Plainlanguage.gov. (2011, May 01). Federal Plain Language Guidelines. Retrieved from https://www.plainlanguage.gov/media/FederalPLGuidelines.pdf

Snow, S. (2015, July 13). How to Write Better Content for Social Media. Retrieved from https://www.socialmediatoday.com/news/how-to-write-better-content-for-social-media/454443/

Vo, K. (2015, June 23). How to Write Social Media Content. Retrieved from https://www.socialmediatoday.com/marketing/kevowriting/2015-06-23/how-write-social-media-content

CHAPTER 8
DRAFT A CONTENT CALENDAR

It's not the sexiest part of your digital strategy, but creating a content calendar is essential for marketing success. It sets you up for internal consistency, promotes flexibility and innovation when it comes to content, and helps your audience know what to expect from your organization and when.

You've already done the work of creating and adapting original content for distribution, and understanding which channels your content is appropriate for. The final step before your content reaches your audience is putting in place a plan for regular (but varied) ways to disperse it. It will take some time and resources, but it's a worthwhile venture.

Content strategist Ahava Leibtag explains, "If you're a content strategist struggling to stay ahead of your deadlines and make sense of your content needs, creating an editorial calendar can help preserve your sanity."

A content calendar will benefit you in many ways:

1. **Strategic goals require strategic tools**

   Content marketing itself is a strategic venture. Decisions about content and its creation happen in terms of big-picture goals and small-scale pivots, which can get confusing. Having an editorial calendar is a place where you can see a panoramic view of your entire content marketing strategy.

2. **Focus allows you to reach your goals**

   In the sometimes scattershot world of social media and digital marketing, it's easy to lose focus, especially if you don't have a large, dedicated team. For many nonprofits, focus is the main challenge when it comes to digital marketing. There is something powerful that happens when you write down your plan: it becomes tangible for everyone, and something to ground yourself with when the strategy gets complicated.

3. **It will make you more consistent**

   Content marketing is *all* about consistency: providing useful content in a consistent manner helps you slowly but surely work your way into the loyal hearts of your customers. If you find your team is losing steam after the first push, a calendar is a great place to double-check that you're following through on promises.

4. **Your team will thank you**

There is a good chance that your team could benefit from better communication. Many teams use such a wide variety of tools that they often have a hard time staying on the same page. A good editorial calendar will bring them to a single place to visualize and execute their shared goals, and provide accountability.

5. **Your audience will love it**

One of the easiest ways to please your audience is to give them something that they'll love on a regular basis. With a calendar, you'll create better content that is more focused on what they need, and is always there at the same time in the same place.

While it often seems like digital marketing is all about speedy climbs to the top of viral charts, slow and steady is a strategy I've seen pay off time and time again. A content calendar helps you be strategic and steady in making sure quality content reaches the right audiences.

How to get started with a calendar

Of course, how you design, share, and access your editorial calendar will ultimately depend on your particular marketing goals and available resources. But at the most fundamental level, I recommend that your editorial calendar include the following fields:

- The date the piece of content will be published
- The topic or headline of the content piece
- The author of the content
- The owner of the content (e.g. who is in charge of making sure the content makes it from ideation to publication and promotion)
- The current status of the content (updated as it moves through your publishing cycle)

Leibtag encourages her clients to create a calendar that goes fairly far into the future: "Don't start small. Your calendar is most effective when you plan six months to a year in advance. Don't go a week or month at a time." She also suggests that organizing a calendar by content type (as well as dates) so that you can you can focus specifically on, for example, what blog posts are going out this week or what Facebook ads.

Depending on your organization's specific goals, your content team's workflow, the formats and platforms with which you plan to work, and the volume of content you will be creating, you may also want to track these elements to help you stay organized and on track over the long term:

- **Content formats**: Is it a blog post? A podcast? An info-graphic? A video? An original image? You might want to consider repurposing pieces of content later on to leverage their full value. Keep track of what formats you have on the go so you'll be able to see what possibilities you haven't tried yet.

- **Channels**: You may include only your owned channels (think your blog, Facebook page, website, YouTube page, email newsletters, etc.) or you can expand your tracking to include paid and earned channels, too.

- **Visuals**: Images are the gold standard in social media market-ing in terms of social sharing potential and overall brand recognition. Tracking the visual elements, such as cover im-ages, logos, illustrations, and charts will help ensure that your work has a cohesive look.

- **Calls to action**: What is your content asking people to do? In-cluding this information in your calendar ensures that every piece of content aligns with your organization's marketing goals.

- **Topic categories**: You want to be able to see at a glance what target topics you've covered often or which you haven't cov-ered enough.

- **Keywords** (and other meta-data): If you have to record which keywords, meta-descriptions and SEO titles (if they differ from your headlines) in the calendar, you'll remember to include them in the content itself.

- **URLs**: Recording your URLs will help when it comes time to do a content audit. Having them easily at hand also makes it easy to link to older pieces of content in the new content you create.

- **Bonus tip**: It may be helpful to have more than one editorial calendar – for example, a master calendar where you can see everything at a glance, and separate calendars for specific activities.

Templates

Anyone with simple Excel skills and an understanding of the organization's bigger content picture can create a customized template.

Your calendar could be organized around timing during the day, as well as days of the week. Or it could be organized around channel and platform. Or it could be organized around theme and message.

A digital content calendar gives you and your team a framework for being deliberate about how you are reaching and building trust with your audience. In part, it is a strategic marketing tool. It is also a place to keep your team organized and on top of things. Both of these things are very important to your digital strategy's success in propelling your organization forward.

Tools for creating content calendars

If you want to go beyond Excel, there is a wide range of tools that have calendaring capabilities that may meet your needs. Many of them are integrated tools meant to help manage the editorial process better.

Some editorial teams use Trello, a free collaboration-management tool that allows a team to track blog categories, article ideas, posts in progress, and published works. Another quality resource is CoSchedule's editorial calendar, blog, and social media planner because it plugs straight into WordPress and integrates with Evernote – easing workflow from initial idea to published blog post.

"Sometimes the best tool isn't the most expensive or complicated. Google Docs is free, easy-to-use, and designed for collaborative editing," writes Helen Nesterenko, founder and CEO of Writtent.com.

My advice would be to keep it simple at first. Use an Excel spreadsheet and share it with the team on Google Docs. Only if you realize you need more firepower should you go to a more complex tool. I have seen many new software tools brought in by managers that never get truly adopted by a team, either because the learning curve is steep or because the tool doesn't match the needs of the team.

Your editorial calendar can help you plan for measurement

You can keep track of the performance of each piece of content. This will give you a head start when it comes time to evaluate the success of your work. It also provides you with concrete numbers at your fingertips to share with your team or upper management.

Should you include page views, clicks, or conversions? You'll need to figure out what the meaningful analytics are for you (see chapter 10 for details) and then add them in as columns (or tabs) in your calendar.

Case Study: Save DC's Kids

CONTENT CALENDAR

Save DC's Kids keeps their content schedule in a Google drive document copied below. It is a living document that is adjusted as the organization measures impact of previous posts and as new events or press opportunities arise.

The Owner column denotes who is responsible for signing off on finished content. It is usually a higher level staff member. The Doer column is the person who is coming up with the content and posting it. It is usually more of a coordinator role. The abbreviations stand for:

SMD: Senior Marketing Manager
MC: Marketing Coordinator
DD: Director of Development

DC: Development Coordinator

VEC: Volunteer Engagement Coordinator

Date	Channel	Content	Owner	Doer
2/5	Facebook & Instagram	Become a Slave Star	VEC	MC
2/6	Instagram	Video interview with parent	SMC	MC
2/6	Email (to all)	Cocktails for Kids Save the Date	DD	DC
2/6	Facebook	#TBT to last year's Cocktails for Kids	DD	DC
2/7	Instagram	Become a Save Star	VEC	MC
2/8	Facebook	Video interview with parent	SMD	MC
2/9	Instagram	Cocktails for Kids Save the Date	DD	DC
2/10	Email (to all)	Become a Save Star	VEC	MC
2/11	n/a	SUNDAY	n/a	n/a
2/12	Facebook & Instagram	Cocktails for Kids Save the Date	DD	DC
2/12	Facebook & Instagram	Snack recipe from Carla Hall	SMD	MC
2/13	Email (nutrition segment)	Snack recipe from Carla Hall	SMD	MC

2/13	Facebook	Infographic with stats on aftercare and employment	SMD	MC
2/14	Facebook & Instagram	We love our Save Stars <3	VEC	MC
2/14	Email (all)	Valentine's Day matching donation	DD	DC
2/15	Instagram	Infographic with stats on aftercare and employment	SMD	MC
2/16	Email (to aftercare segment)	Infographic with stats on aftercare and employment	SMD	MC

DRAFT A CONTENT CALENDAR

	TOPIC/TITLE	CONTENT	PLATFORM(S)	TARGET PERSONA(S)	CALL TO ACTION
MONDAY Author: Owner: Due Date: Publish Date:					
TUESDAY Author: Owner: Due Date: Publish Date:					
WEDNESDAY Author: Owner: Due Date: Publish Date:					
THURSDAY Author: Owner: Due Date: Publish Date:					
FRIDAY Author: Owner: Due Date: Publish Date:					

REFERENCES

Leibtag, A. (2014). *The Digital Crown: Winning at Content on the Web*. Waltham, MA: Morgan Kaufmann.

Nesterenko, H. (2017, March 29). Top 15 Life-Changing Editorial Calendar Tools. Retrieved from https://writtent.com/blog/15-life-changing-editorial-calendar-tools/

CHAPTER 9
PLAN YOUR RESOURCES

I always tell my kids not to bite off more than they can chew. No, literally. That peanut butter rice cake is just too big. The same goes for a digital strategy. It's easy to look at a large organization online and say, "Let's do that." but for small- to mid-sized organizations, a plan like that almost always ends in disaster.

Whatever new tactics you decide to employ – whether it's partnerships with influencers, revamped email campaigns, or a serious video strategy – it must be appropriate for the number of **people** you have on hand with the right skills, the kinds of **software resources** you want to invest in, and the amount of **money** you're putting behind it.

Not every organization can – or should – emulate the large-scale moves of, say, an international organization with a significant endowment. Instead, think Goldilocks: there's a strategy out there that is the just the right size for your organization's particular needs. And knowing that you have the resources to actually own and execute your strategy will only strengthen it.

Caleb Sexton of Maga Design says that knowing what resources you need to make your strategy a success is mission critical:

> A strategy can only be successful if, and only if, it is action-oriented. When we work with our clients to build out their strategy we often ask them what does success look like in their eyes. From that vision, we go back to today and facilitate a series of structured co-creation sessions with them and their team to build strategic roadmaps to visualize what's required to get there. This is often done on a large wall plot, using sticky notes, a pre-defined working canvas, and a facilitator to help keep the team moving forward. In such situations, it's necessary to help them define and decide what key activities, milestones, and resources will be needed for success. When such a session is over we then work with our design team to visualize the roadmap as a referenceable artifact. As the strategy begins to be executed we update the map as needed to reflect changes, pivots, or new information.

People

In a recent study, fifty-seven percent of charities cite skills (or lack thereof) as being the biggest barrier to getting more from a digital strategy.

> Sixty-six percent are worried that they will miss out on opportunities for digital fundraising. If their board and leadership team do not increase their digital skills, more than half are worried about giving competitors an advantage (53%), losing touch with their audience (53%) or their charity becoming irrelevant (53%).

First, look at the people you already have on your team. This includes staff, partners, and to an extent, volunteers. How much time are they already spending on their day-to-day tasks, and how much time can they contribute to a digital strategy?

Remember that journey map? Hopefully you now have a grasp on what your customer or audience touchpoints will look like and the content that needs to be created, delivered, and measured. So now, the question is: who is going to get it all done?

When it comes to implementing a digital strategy, I like to think of the people driving success in three categories: ownership, creation, and delivery.

The owner is the person who needs to make sure the work is done and the person who is tracking the whole process. This individual may be a strategist, a project manager, or a senior executive. It needs to be someone who will ultimately take ownership of the campaign and be responsible for the operation of it. If there's a problem, the owner is the person who ultimately needs to address it. If there's a win, she can take credit. Ideally, the owner needs to be able to flag issues that come up, bring in additional resources as needed, manage a budget (to an extent), and develop updates and reports for the leadership of the organization.

The creator may be different for each piece of content within a campaign or strategy. For example, a creator may be a graphic designer for an infographic, a content writer for a blog post, or a video producer for a short web video. Whatever is needed to execute the strategy, you will need to build your team of creators. Often, these individuals can be outside your organization – contractors or third-part vendors – who offer a level of expertise that can be leveraged for your digital campaign.

Finally, the delivery person may be a member of your team who is responsible for scheduling and/or implementing the work. This is essentially the person that is hitting the enter key and sending out posts, publishing web content, and blasting out email campaigns. Ideally this person is in regular contact with the creators and the owner. She knows when an item is approved and uses the content calendar (or some other system) to make sure she has a green light before posting or publishing. The delivery can be accomplished using outside software for scheduled posts, a content management system (CMS), or it can be done manually.

Software

Software can make the implementation and measurement of your digital strategy more efficient. Software can also display your reports in a pretty format. No, seriously. Many third-party tools out there now synthesize your analytics and pull together reporting in a way that is beautiful to look at and much easier to understand. Good reporting will serve you well in high-level presentations to senior staff or top leadership of an organization.

Let's get back to the efficiency piece for a moment. Using third-party software to house and schedule posts are also ways to track and monitor your engagement with those posts. It helps your team stay on the same page, and it helps you understand how successful you are with engaging your audience.

Your technology infrastructure will support both external and internal communications. You'll need tools to manage your digital marketing properties and tactics, but you will also need ones for internal functions such as email, document storage and more. This book is primarily targeted to marketing professionals, not technology professionals, so I will only touch on the basics of the requirements for a proper technology infrastructure. There are many factors that go into these technology decisions, but it is important that the digital marketing team understands the pieces and how they relate to realizing marketing goals, connecting with audiences, and providing measurements of success.

But what do you really need?

Technology changes fast. Your needs evolve. Companies that create software are acquired or go out of business. Sometimes products become outdated – or something new and better appears.

I don't often recommend specific software unless I know the needs of an organization, but I felt that for those who wanted an idea of the kinds of things many organizations use, I could provide a list:

<u>A good all-in-one tool</u>:

HubSpot is an inbound marketing and sales platform that helps companies attract visitors, convert leads, and close customers.

"With straightforward dashboards, you can see at a glance exactly how your website, social media channels, landing pages and calls to action are doing – how many visits they've had and where those visitors have come from, how you're doing in comparison to competitors, and how many inbound links you're getting," according to SplitPixel Creative, an established digital marketing and web design agency. "It also has some simple SEO tools to help you monitor how you're ranking, and how much traffic you're getting, from specific keywords."

For customer relationship management (CRM)/integrated approach: **Salesforce** is a complete suite of business applications. It allows one to monitor and manage everything from sales leads to support tickets, and from channel marketing to website analytics.

For social media:
Facebook Insights provides a lot of the metrics that you'll need. Software such as **Sprout Social** or **Hootsuite** collects them in one place and can be more adjustable.

Using Hootsuite's reporting functions, you can take benefit from real-time analytics of social media metrics, such as including followers, mentions, engagement, clicks on links in your content, and the performance of your social media team in responding to messages. With Hootsuite, it's also easy to demonstrate the ROI of your social platforms.

For social listening:
Keyhole is a real-time hashtag tracker for Twitter, Instagram and Facebook. **Mention** is a tool that allows one to monitor key phrases and organization names in real time.

For your website:

Google Analytics offers free and enterprise analytics tools to measure website, app, digital and offline data to gain customer insights.

Google Analytics offers user-friendly tools to monitor and report on bounce rates, conversions, page views, visitor acquisition and segmentation. All of these basic metrics demonstrate whether your digital marketing activity is thriving or running out of steam. Google Analytics is probably the most straightforward tool you can use for reporting on pay-per-click (PPC) campaigns as it integrates directly with AdWords, and you can also use e-commerce reporting to monitor sales activity and performance.

For email marketing:

MailChimp is one of my favorite email marketing platforms. It's easy to use and it gives you access to an array of email marketing tools all conveniently located in one place. Its interface is user-friendly and produces elegant emails without graphic design experience. We'll see if another player disrupts this space, but for now I'm bananas for the 'Chimp.

For mobile:

Mixpanel allows you to see how people use your app with advanced mobile and web analytics.

Mixpanel is a high-quality tool for mobile, allowing you to measure the ways people are using your app or site. For example, you can check whether people are returning and using them again after their first visit. You can also receive insights into the functions that make people most likely to give up in the process of using your app or site – potentially losing you customers. Mixpanel also offers a straightforward method of carrying out A/B testing in apps and websites, so that you can directly measure the success of your new plan compared to how you were conducting activities before.

Money

Let's just address the elephant in the room. How much should your organization be spending on digital marketing? I'll get to that answer in a moment, but let's first examine why it's important to budget for marketing, or how you can make the case to your top leadership.

For nonprofits, it's a lot easier to ask for money when someone knows what you stand for, is already familiar with your organization, and trusts you. Digital marketing allows people to get to know your organization and its values. Digital marketing done right will have a good return on investment. On the other side of the coin, you may need to reach out to the people who need your services – digital marketing is also a great way to find and connect with those people.

How much should you be spending? Three percent of your total operating budget, give or take. A comprehensive study by the

American Marketing Association and Lipman Hearne found that the average non-profit marketing budget was between two and three percent of the total operating budget.

Non-profits lag behind for-profit companies in spending on marketing. According to a study from The CMO Survey and Deloitte Digital, for-profit companies on average spend 7.5 percent of total revenue on marketing.

John Suart, author, consultant, and expert in nonprofit marketing, writes, "It is tempting to think that the non-profit world's marketing and communications budgets should mirror the for-profit world. A case can be made that in fact non-profits need to spend more than for-profits on marketing, not less. However, everything points to the fact that the sector would have little appetite for such a radical increase."

There are arguments to be made for spending more on marketing. More marketing can have a direct effect on increased donations. It can help the recipients of your organization's services find you and thus make your efforts more effective. But it can be difficult for an organization that wants to get the lion's share of each dollar to the recipient to allocate more to marketing. Donors want to fund programs, not promotion.

Let's talk about what three percent, give or take, looks like in practice. Here are examples from John Suart: if a charity had an operating budget of $500,000, its base marketing and communications budget would be $15,000. If it had an operating budget of $5 million, it would be $150,000.

Once you've created your overall budget, you will need to assess how much is needed for specific campaigns and perhaps even specific pieces of content. A video can cost $500, $5,000, or $50,000 to produce. So, make sure you can point to your goals and deliver a return on your investment.

Don't get too distracted by the bells and whistles

The purpose of your marketing is to get real people out in the world to do something. That is its core value. Sometimes one can get caught up in how cool or creative we can be, which is fun, but it doesn't matter if it isn't providing results. Legendary ad man David Ogilvy has a maxim: "If it doesn't sell, it isn't creative." It is a good reminder to invest your marketing dollars where they can work the hardest for you, not in the prettiest new thing.

One of the unsexy but totally necessary parts of marketing is distribution. You need to get your message in front of people. Jack E. Kosakowski, CEO of Junior Achievement USA, writes, "If you have a limited budget, don't make the mistake of spending 90 percent of it on the 'creative' and then have no money to distribute it… Be sure to allocate some resources – whether it be a modest budget, in-kind support of ad space, or some combination of both – to get your message distributed to your key audiences."

Kosakowski celebrates the low-cost marketing resources and distribution methods on the Internet, including email platforms, digital advertising solutions, social media management tools, analytic resources, and SEO apps. "Be sure to take the time to research these kinds of resources and use them whenever possible. It's an investment of time, but a wise one for a nonprofit with limited marketing dollars," writes Kosakowski.

How to allocate your marketing budget

How much of your budget should be spent on digital marketing? And on which tactics?

You may have noticed that throughout this book, I keep suggesting that you circle back to your goals. I'm going to do it again: your budget depends on what you hope to achieve and having as complete a vision as you can about what you want to do to achieve it. Adam Fifield, head of content marketing at Leadgenix, writes, "You can't set your PPC budget without actually thinking about what campaigns you're going to be running, what they'll look like, and the price range your keywords might fall in." It's true.

You should look at the marketing efforts you've made already and see what worked. Analyze past efforts. Fifield writes, "What strategies did you spend your money on last year? And of those, which ones were most successful? Which ones were duds?" He suggests that you allocate money according to what is successful rather than how much a strategy costs. "Even though posting to Twitter is technically free, if Twitter marketing is working well for you, you want to toss some more money at that initiative," writes Fifield. He also suggests that you allocate 20 percent of your budget to trying new things.

What are other organizations in your field doing? When you are thinking about allocating your resources, it can only help for you to learn from other people's mistakes and successes. If you are still using direct mail, while others in your field are connecting online, you may want to try the same thing.

But what is the ballpark percentage of a marketing budget that should go to digital marketing? Fifield writes, "Ten to 50 percent of your total marketing budget should be used for digital. Once a digital marketing budget baseline has been established, the budget is divided into four areas: SEO, PPC, social media, and content marketing."

Case Study: Save DC's Kids

RESOURCES

<u>Save DC's Kids' People</u>

Senior Marketing Manager

Save brought Susan Gold onto its team about five years ago and they haven't looked back since. Susan supervises the organization's marketing coordinator and is responsible for architecting the overall marketing strategy of the organization, evaluating it and making high level changes based on what's working and what isn't. This includes event publicity and traditional communications work as well as digital strategy. She works closely with the development team as well as the Save DC digital strategy consultant and board members. Susan's background is in political campaign marketing and she cut her teeth on races in Iowa, Pennsylvania, Virginia and Ohio.

Marketing Coordinator

Susan works directly with Tom Kelly, Save's marketing coordinator. Tom helps Susan develop the Save marketing plan and then implements the plan. He also manages vendor relationships such as with Save's graphic designer and nonprofit technology specialist, as well as email marketing points of contact. He collaborates closely with the development department and volunteer engagement staff person. Lastly, Tom is responsible for day-to-day evaluation of the Save marketing strategy and keeping Susan informed of all metrics and overall trends.

Director of Development

Andrew Wagner is Save's Director of Development. His focus is on foundation and major donors, as well as individual and online giving. He reports directly to the Save Executive Director. A portion of his compensation is tied to how much he raises annually. Andrew's previous experience is in the world of theater and the arts, first fundraising for Wolftrap and then for the Studio Theater. He worked closely with the Senior Marketing Manager and supervises the Development Coordinator, who is also on his team.

Development Coordinator

When Director of Development Andrew first started at Save in 2014, the development team at Save was a shop of one. He quickly fundraised to cover the salary of a second staff person and welcomed Stacey Fitzgerald onto his team. Stacey graduated from American University in 2015 and joined the Save team immediately thereafter. She processes all individual donations, ensures individual donors are properly and promptly thanked, and is responsible for keeping Salesforce up to date. Lastly, Stacey plans Save's annual fundraiser, Cocktails for Kids.

Volunteer Engagement Coordinator

Ruth Hess is Save's volunteer guru. Although her position is a salaried role on staff now, she started as a Save Star in 2014 and was offered a full-time role in 2016. This was a tough decision for Ruth as she was a retiree, but the power of Save's mission lured her out of retirement and back into the ranks of the nonprofit sector. Hess coordinates all volunteer recruitment and training, and works very closely with the current and past Save Star volunteers.

Digital Strategist (Consultant)

After a few years of managing their entire digital strategy in house, Save made the decision to bring on a digital strategy consultant, Eve Lee, to advise on big picture online marketing plans and help the organization make periodic adjustments to the strategy based on key metrics on a quarterly basis. Prior to working with Eve, Save hired a consultant who was part of a large firm and had expertise in early childhood education policy. Eve is Save's current consultant and she's a one-woman show. Eve has a modest retainer with Save for the 2017 calendar year.

Graphic Designer (Consultant)

Jennifer King is Save's graphic design consultant. She produces all the visual materials the organization needs, from social media images to event invites to infographics to annual reports. She works on an hourly basis out of her home in Richmond, VA.

Nonprofit Technology Specialist (Consultant)

One of the folks Susan Gold suggested to Save when she started was a small contract with a technology specialist to train new and existing employees on Salesforce and other online tools. Since Save isn't large enough to have an IT department, they decided to work with Stuart Hernandez as both a trainer and technical implementer as needed. Stuart has several other clients and specializes in cloud-based CRM solutions. He used to work for Constant Contact before striking out on his own.

<u>Save DC's Kids' Money</u>

Salaries and consultant's fees:
In order to implement their online marketing strategy, Save has set aside a significant percentage of their general operating budget for salaries and fees to cover working with consultants. They've secured special funding for this year's increased focus on digital strategy from foundations and major donors.

Here's how the numbers break down:
- Senior Marketing Manager: $83,000/year
- Marketing Coordinator: $59,000/year
- Director of Development: $91,000
- Development Coordinator: $63,000/year
- Volunteer Engagement Coordinator: $55,000/year

- Digital Strategist (Consultant): $4,000/month for 12 months
- Graphic Designer (Consultant): $75/hour for 3-7 hours/month
- Nonprofit Technology Specialist (Consultant): $50/hour for 5 hours/month

Boosted FB and Instagram Posts -- The organization has also set aside a full $7,000 to pay for social media advertising in the form of boosted Facebook posts, Facebook ads, and Instagram ads. This may seem like quite a large amount of money, but the organization has seen some very significant results using these channels in the past and knows they need to spend money to meet their aggressive growth goals.

Wealth Screening: $350/month for a LexisNexis subscription
Email Marketing: $196/month for VerticalResponse subscription

Save DC's Kids' Technology
Salesforce (Customer Relationship Management)
VerticalResponse (Email Marketing)
LexisNexis (Wealth Screening)

PLAN YOUR RESOURCES

TIME	PEOPLE	SOFTWARE
TOTAL HOURS /MONTH:	**TOTAL COST:**	**TOTAL COST:**

REFERENCES

Fifield, A. (2017). 5 Tips to Nail Down This Year's Digital Marketing Budget. Retrieved from https://mention.com/blog/digital-marketing-budget/

Kosakowski, J. (2017, February 14). Building Your Brand On A Nonprofit Budget. Retrieved from https://www.forbes.com/sites/forbesnonprofitcouncil/2017/02/14/building-your-brand-on-a-nonprofit-budget/#2048e09f3a65

Sexton, C. (2017, July 19). Phone interview

Splitpixel Creative. (2016, September 13). The seven best tools for measuring the success of your digital marketing plan. Retrieved from http://www.splitpixel.co.uk/blog/seven-best-tools-measuring-success-digital-plan/

Suart, J. C. (2011, October). 3% Give or Take: Non-Profit Marketing & Communications Budget Benchmark. Retrieved from http://www.johnsuart.com/3P-Give-or-Take.pdf

CHAPTER 10
SIMPLY MEASURE

The last piece of your digital strategy is figuring out if your efforts are working. Are you getting the results you hoped for? Are you reaching your goals?

To answer these questions, you need to measure the impact of your campaign. You need to study analytics and collect data pertinent to your efforts. Take a moment to appreciate that you are marketing now and not 30 years ago. Collecting data is easier in the digital sphere than ever before. Indeed, the problem now might be that we collect too much data and then have a difficult time telling what is most meaningful.

The analytics that you collect should be rooted in your original goals. Remember the goals you set out at the beginning of your strategy? The ones that align with your organization's core values? Those meaningful, manageable and measurable goals? They've guided you through the whole process and they will guide you through measurement as well.

If your analytics aren't rooted in your goals, they are arbitrary. They are fluff.

What kind of key performance indicators (KPIs) should you use?

Each of your goals should have a Key Performance Indicator, or KPI. "A KPI is a measurable value that demonstrates how effectively a company is achieving key business objectives," according to Klipfolio, a software company that offers dynamic, web-based dashboards.

Mark Kelly, author at Salsa Labs, made a list of the most common KPIs for nonprofits and organized them into four categories: fundraising, donor retention, email and social media. Not all of these KPIs will be appropriate for your organization, but they might help you think about what metrics are the best fit to your goals.

Fundraising metrics

1. **Gifts Secured**: "The name says it all," writes Kelly. "Gifts secured simply accounts for how many gifts your organization received over a set amount of time." The amount of time is up to you, though it makes sense to collect data throughout a digital campaign to track its effectiveness.

You might also split this measurement up between gift types. For example, if you are trying to develop a major gift program, you might want to isolate major gifts.

Keeping track of your gifts secured in real time can help you figure out if you are meeting your short-term goals. Real time measurement will also help you adjust your digital campaign if your numbers aren't good before you go too far off track.

To calculate: add up how many gifts your organization received over a certain period of time. The sum equals your gifts secured.

2. **Donation Growth**: This metric tracks your gift secured over a longer span of time. This can help ensure that you're meeting your long-term fundraising goals.

Are you getting more donations now than you were a year ago? More now than before you started your digital campaign? Do you see any patterns in gifts secured over time?

If you notice there are times of year when growth is stagnant, you can make plans to increase growth at those times next year.

To calculate: as with gifts secured, add up how many gifts your organization received over a certain period of time.

3. **Average Gift Size Growth**: This metric measures the percentage by which your average gift size has increased (let's hope) over a certain period of time.

In a fundraising effort, you can try to increase the number of people that donate, but you can also try to increase the size of each gift. Consider leveraging your relationships and spend less time focusing on finding new donors. Instead, spend more time cultivating your current relationships for maximum benefit.

After all, if you receive $10,000 from five people, that's the same amount of money as getting $1,000 from 50 people.

To calculate: divide the sum of your donations last year by total number of donations last year. Repeat with this year's donations. Subtract last year's average from this year's average. Then, divide the difference by last year's average. Multiply by 100 to calculate your percent increase.

4. **Fundraising Return on Investment (ROI)**: How many fundraising dollars come in per dollars spent on fundraising? For any project, you should keep track of your return on investment. This is especially important for an organization with a limited budget.

Using this metric is essential because it demonstrates how well your marketing campaign and fundraising efforts are working. If it's a good number, you can use it to promote your efforts to other people in your organization so that they can support your work.

In this case, you would want your funds raised to be greater than your costs. Just be flexible during the process, since in most cases there will be room for improvement. If you can continue lowering your costs, the amount of money you can put directly towards your cause will be even greater.

To calculate: Divide your total costs by total funds raised. If your result is less than 1, your organization gained more than it spent. If it's greater than 1, you spent more than you gained.

5. **Online Gift Percentage**: What portion of your overall donations have come from online channels? This is a KPI that shows the success of your digital fundraising.

In most cases, the cost of acquiring donations online is much lower than through any other medium. At the end of the day, you want to maintain a healthy percentage of gifts received digitally.

Fundraising software can track all gifts, which can make it easy to see how many of your gifts were made online and how many offline.

To calculate: Divide the number of total online gifts received this year by total number of gifts. Multiply by 100.

Donor retention metrics

Acquisition of donors is good, but it won't ultimately grow your organization if most of your supporters only give once and don't return. Donor retention is often undervalued, but it is crucial to the success of many organizations.

Without solid donor retention, the focus of the acquisition will have to be on recovery rather than progress. Ideally, you want to put more of your concentration on forward progress.

1. **Donor Retention Rate**: This metric is the percentage of donors who have given more than once.

Recurring donors are incredibly valuable to nonprofits. "In fact, about 88 percent of funds raised come from only 12 percent of an organization's donor base," writes Kelly. "A whopping 87 percent of those funds are made by recurring donors. Now you can see for yourself: acquiring new relationships is always more costly than cultivating existing ones.

To calculate: Divide the number of recurring donors by total number of donors, then multiply by 100.

2. **Donor Growth (Year-Over-Year)**: How much has your donor base grown (or shrunk) over a year?

This metric may reveal that your issue is with acquisition and not retention. The most thorough way of thinking about your donor base is to look at a bunch of donor KPIs together. Are you getting new donors? Are you keeping your old ones?

To calculate: Divide the total number of donors in your base at the end of last year by the total number of donors in your base this year. Multiply by 100.

3. **Recurring Gift Percentage**: This metric tells your organization exactly what portion of your total gifts come from recurring donors. Like donor retention, this metric is important because recurring gifts are more important to most organizations than one-time gifts.

If you can confidently expect that you'll continue to receive those gifts and recognize where those gifts are coming from, you may want to consider leveraging this aspect. In this case, it is recommended to begin a small, targeted campaign to increase those gift sizes.

To calculate: divide number of recurring gifts by total number of gifts received. Multiply by 100.

4. **Giving Capacity**: This metric is an informed estimate of how much money your donors are able to give.

Knowing the giving capacity of donors allows your organization to make more specific and relevant asks. When coupled with additional data sources – such as giving history – you can approximately forecast how much your organization might receive from donors over a given year. Knowing the giving capacity gives you a better idea of how much to ask for.

Another note on this: if you have a group of donors who give large amounts, you might want to keep track of them separately. They may require different kinds of communication than donors who make smaller donations.

To measure: for this one, you'll need the assistance of a prospect research and wealth screening software such as iWave or DonorSearch.

5. **Conversion Rate:** This metric tells you how many donors took an action when prompted by your organization. Look at a specific call to action? How many people did it? It shows you if your outreach is effective. It will also help you better understand the habit and affinities of your audience, which will help you next time you want to engage to do so better.

It can be more informative to look at the conversion rate for calls to action that don't include asks for donation. Your relationships with your donors run deeper than simply requesting and receiving donations. With this in mind, it's important to determine that you're engaging your donors beyond the donation process.

To measure: divide total number of donors who took an action by total donors prompted by the CTA. Multiply by 100.

6. **Outreach Rate**: This metric shows how often you're getting in touch with your donors. How often are you using a specific channel? Regular outreach is an important part of keeping your audience engaged.

To measure: count how many times you contacted donors through one or more channels over a certain amount of time.

Email metrics

According to Kelly, one-third of online funds are raised through emails, so he suggests having metrics related directly to the optimization of email marketing.

1. **Open Rate**: These metrics shows you the percentage of recipients who opened an email from your organization.

This is important to keep in mind because if your donors are not bothering to open your emails, then the engagement process is over before it even starts. Potential donors won't see all of the amazing content you're sharing about your cause or have the opportunity to donate if they don't get a chance to see your riveting content.

If your open rate is low, you should experiment with subject lines. Most email marketing software allows you to split test your emails.

By doing this, you can test the efficacy of different subject lines and choose the line most likely to elicit higher open rates.

Also make sure that the email address from which you are sending your emails is recognizable to the recipients. Do you open emails from unknown addresses? Other people don't either.

To measure: email marketing software will automatically track open rates for you.

2. **Click Through Rate (CTR)**: This metric shows what percentage of recipients clicked on a link included in your email.

CTR is an effective way of determining how many supporters took the next step by visiting your website, your online donation page, or another important link.

To measure: This is another KPI tracked by email marketing software.

3. **Email Conversion Rate**: The metric will show how many of your recipients followed through with your call to action.

"If it turns out your email conversion is lower than you would have liked, one of the easiest fixes is tweaking your call-to-action," explains Kelly. "Make sure it's clear and easy to spot so that donors know exactly what you're asking for and how to act accordingly."

To measure: This is a metric that your email marketing software will calculate for you. However, if you want to calculate it on your own, simply divide the total number of people contacted by the total number of actions taken, then multiply by 100.

4. **Opt-Out Rate**: This metric measures how many recipients in your list unsubscribed from your email campaign over a certain amount of time.

Often if you email too often, you'll have higher opt-out rates. Some types of content might also be a turn off for your audience. Is it providing something of value to your recipients?

To measure: provided by your email marketing software.

Social media metrics

What social media metrics are most often relevant to nonprofit organizations? We kept the best for last here. Often there is an overemphasis on impressions, when what you should focus on instead is engagement.

"You want to drive your followers to your website, not simply collect 'likes' on your Facebook page. In fact, pure social media reach on some platforms, like Facebook, may be a lot less valuable than you might think," writes Kelly.

Kelly suggests that you try to send more prospects from social media to your website, where you'll be able to convert them and gather valuable information. It is also important, in the age of low organic reach on social media platforms, to encourage your followers to share your content.

1. **Amplification, Applause, and Conversation Rates**:
These three metrics are more meaningful as a unit.

Amplification refers to when a third party shares social media posts. Think retweets, shares, revines, repins or reblogs. The better your amplification, the greater your reach.

Applause refers to when someone interacts with your content in a relatively passive way. It's a like or a heart or whatever other emoji. "Applause rate is like amplification-lite," writes Kelly. "You won't learn much more than what people like and don't like from applause rate."

Conversation refers to when your post starts a chain of interactions. Think comments or replies on Twitter.

Conversations allow supporters to tell you exactly what they're interested in directly from their own mouths. This allows you to post relevant content that's going to spark conversations.

Read comments. They will help you optimize your social media outreach and may give you ideas about other things that your organization does. Look at these metrics together to figure out what your social network wants from you.

To calculate: the "Insights" or analytics section of each social media platform will provide this kind of information, as will software like Sprout Social or Tweetdeck, among others.

2. **Landing Page Conversion Rate**: This metric measures how many visitors to your donation page – in this case, from social media – completed the donation process.

By using a tracking tool, such as Google Analytics, you can determine how many visitors reached a specific page, how they arrived there, and how many completed the action on that page.

To calculate: divide total number of visitors to your donation page by total number of donations made. Multiply by 100.

3. **Fundraiser Participation Rate**: This metric tracks how many of your fundraisers are working to secure donations on your behalf and what actions they're taking to do so. If you do peer-to-peer fundraising, this will be an important metric for you.

Look at how much money each fundraiser has raised. Then also note where and how often fundraisers took actions to participate in your campaign. By viewing these two metrics together, you can determine how successful the efforts of individual fundraisers were and how much work you should put into to put into your campaign.

To measure: enlist the help of a great peer-to-peer software, which will automatically track fundraiser actions and allow you to oversee participation.

What kind of metrics should you be wary of?

You've been cautioned not to become overwhelmed by too many numbers and to make sure you are collecting meaningful metrics. In my experience, the mistake that some organizations make is that they use numbers that aren't appropriately contextualized. Traffic reports might not be fine grained enough to tell you if you are meeting your organization's actual goals. Facebook likes are fine, but if they don't correspond with more engagement, they might not mean much for you.

You need to have context to know if you can use your numbers to make decisions. For example, if you create a $10,000 video and it nets you 100 new Facebook likes, then the metrics suggest that your ROI is not great. But if you get 100 new Facebook likes organically without a big spend, that might show that you have a healthy community on Facebook and your content is getting shared.

Another example of a metric that requires context to be meaningful is bounce rate. Most people feel that a lower bounce rate is better. But that depends on how people are using your website. If they are clicking around a lot and staying on a page because they can't find the information they need, then a low bounce rate might not mean that your overall goals are being met. Conversely, sometimes a higher bounce rate will reflect the fact that visitors were able to come to your website, get the info they needed, complete a task quickly, and then leave. Efficiency can, without context, appear to be a high bounce rate.

Another word of warning: don't expect digital marketing results to happen immediately. Like any outreach work, it takes some time. It can move only as fast as people's attention and behavior allow. According to SplitPixel Creative, a digital marketing and web design agency in the United Kingdom, "Metrics don't necessarily show a return on investment straight away, and this is a big part of why many digital marketers run into problems convincing decision makers in their organization of the importance of search or content marketing – they're expecting a different measure of success."

You've got your analytics, now what?
How you report your numbers is important. You need to share your findings in a way that is meaningful to your organization. To make them meaningful, your reports should align with your goals.

Furthermore, a report should be actionable. Pair your measurements with recommendations to improve. What is working? Capitalize on that. What isn't working? Do you need to pivot to another tactic? Your report should show clearly what you've learned so that decisions can be made about what to do next.

Good reporting can help build confidence among stakeholders. Doing it regularly allows you to have a living, breathing strategy that can respond to changing circumstances. You don't want your strategy to be set in stone from the beginning; instead, you want it to grow in response to how well it works. Flexibility is key. Not only does the market change, but your priorities as an organization may also change.

I recommend creating a custom dashboard that is user-friendly and intuitive for a layperson. It should also provide you with constant updates. In addition, the dashboard should include only the metrics that are meaningful for you and should be accessible to everyone involved in your digital marketing strategy.

I also recommend that there is some clear ownership for your digital strategy that appoints a person who is responsible on checking in on the metrics on a continual basis. As the digital world changes, your strategy will evolve. The process needs to be looked at and documented.

Another aspect of measurement is that what you measure ends up having specific incentives for your stakeholders and may affect how you do things in unexpected ways. We've seen the negative effects of online publishers who are hungry for clicks alone: fluffy clickbait. Black hat SEO is an example of how a certain incentive system has caused people to do things that otherwise wouldn't make sense. A friend worked at a company that put financial incentives in places related to traffic on blog posts written and socialized by different team members. The management team hoped that overall numbers would go up and each team member would work to the best of their capacity, but instead the competition between team members caused them to socialize some blog posts at the expense of others. The take-home message: be mindful that what you measure affects how you do your work.

How do other people measure the success of a campaign?
When Hager Sharp worked with the National Board for Professional Teaching Standards (NBPTS), the firm wanted to recruit teachers to participate in the field test and sign up to "test drive" components of the recently revised National Board assessment. The audience was hyper-targeted – comprising a mix of teachers in specific curriculum areas and spanning multiple grade levels, including primarily teachers who were not yet certified.

To be successful, Hager Sharp had to overcome several barriers, including a short timeline and an extensive sign-up process that included an eight-page form.

Given the objective to drive measurable action by a narrow audience in a short timeframe, Hager Sharp developed a paid digital advertising plan that included a diverse mix of publishers – including multiple ad networks, Facebook, Google search, and Monster.com – and strong audience targeting.

Once live, Hager Sharp closely monitored campaign performance, and online publishers were adjusted based on whether they delivered test application completions (or conversions), which resulted in the removal of low-performing publishers mid-flight and the addition of new ones.

Hager Sharp also closely monitored visitor behavior upon arrival at the campaign landing page. After the first week of the campaign, the firm noted that the vast majority of users were leaving without completing the application. They reviewed the site analytics data to understand where users were encountering challenges and, combining these insights with a deep understanding of website user experience best practices, worked with the National Board to implement changes to ensure visitors could easily complete the form. As a result of these revisions, the campaign saw a positive decline in the cost per conversion. Overall, it resulted in nearly 2,000 completed registrations and exceeded their click-through rate and cost per click goals.

The National Board re-engaged Hager Sharp to drive registration to the second phase of the field test. Hager Sharp selected the two highest performing channels from the previous year – Facebook and Google search – to ensure cost-effective conversions. Using the same high-touch monitoring, they adjusted budget and publishers throughout the campaign to ensure cost-effective conversions. As a result, the second effort successfully converted more than double the registrations as the first (4,300+) and at a low cost per conversion.

In addition, Hager Sharp worked with the National Board to market its web-based video case library, ATLAS, to instructional leaders and administrators at the district level, as well as within teacher prep programs at colleges and universities.

Among other activities, Hager Sharp produced and promoted via YouTube a documentary-style video featuring Northwestern State University, and promoted two blog posts targeting educators and administrators via LinkedIn. YouTube advertising of the documentary produced 113,827 views among Pre-K to 12th grade teachers and administrators at a cost per view of $0.03 – one-third of YouTube's average cost per view of $0.10. The LinkedIn campaign to promote the blog posts earned more than 175,000 impressions and nearly 1,200 engagements.

What does success look like for you?

I asked Caleb Sexton of Maga Design about how his organization measures success. Sexton went on to explain:

> Success for us is a mix of qualitative and quantitative feedback. A big driver of it however is focused on adoption and buy-in throughout an organization. Much of our work is dedicated to helping drive strategy across an organization as much as it is to see how it manifests outside in the market. This is often in the form of engagement, buy-in, alignment and satisfaction regarding change tracked over time. This doesn't so much as show up in day as it does over year or two years.

I recently read an article on Docurated about how different marketing professionals quantify success. There were thirty marketers included in the article and they gave thirty different answers.

"The most important key metric to track when measuring the effectiveness of your marketing campaign is the cost to acquire a single new customer [or donor]," writes Joseph Hirschhorn Howard, senior marketing manager at Masslight in Washington, D.C. "This simple statistic will help you evaluate the overall rate of growth of your business [or organization]. If the cost to find, convince, and onboard new customers is too high, your business won't be viable in the long-term. There are other metrics that are also highly important, but this one will provide a telling view from 30,000 feet."

"Tools like 'Optimizely' allow one to AB test different elements on a website and let the users vote on the effectiveness of a micro-marketing initiative with their behavioral patterns," claims Nima Noori, CEO of TorontoVaporizer. "If the color of a sign-up button changes and the click through rate goes up by one percent, that may indicate that the new color is just more effective. This is the new era of marketing that is driven by real-time data and users voting with their behavior."

"All of my marketing efforts are measured against business goals, and I use a mix of tools and metrics to do that. For instance, if brand awareness is a goal, I will track the reach and engagement of my social media posts in the platform analytics and in my 3rd party tools like Sprout Social," writes Michelle Stinson Ross, head of Outreach at AuthorityLabs.

What success looks like for you is dependent on your goals. Are you getting the donations you need to do the important work that you do? Are you finding the service users that are most in need and incorporating them into your programming? Are you providing the services that best solve the social problem that your organization wants to address?

Case Study: Save DC's Kids

MEASUREMENT

Save DC's Kids used the goals they created back at the beginning of their fiscal year to build out a measurement plan. To recap, the organization is looking for:

1. 10,000 new social media followers/email housefile members
2. 1,000 new donors
3. 100 super volunteers (aka Save Stars)

Social Media Followers and Housefile Members

Save has been around for over 20 years and their email, social media and volunteer populations are large. Their measurement plan and goals are as follows for their 12-month strategy outlined in this book:

4,000 new email addresses
Save's current email list hovers near 21,000 addresses and their goal is expanding it to 25,000 names in one year. Save will also need to account for the expected 13-14 percentage churn of folks who will leave their list annually.

End of year update: although it had a lofty goal, Save was able to reach the 25,000 mark for its number of email addresses in its

VerticalResponse housefile just before the clock hit midnight on 12/31. The triple gift match Save launched in early December gave them the boost they needed to increase their list size. During a particularly nervous moment in September, the suggestion was made that the organization buy email addresses from a partner organization. But upon further research, this was considered significantly too expensive.

3,000 new Facebook fans
Save boasts 8,754 Facebook fans today. Increasing this number by 3,000 will take a thoughtful strategy, powerful messaging, and a budget to ensure Save's content gets in front of new potential fans.

One mistake Save made during their 2015 strategy was to focus only on Facebook fans and not on other meaningful online interactions (such as email list sign-ups or donations). Note that the organization's strategy includes metrics in addition to the Facebook fan number to avoid making this mistake again.

End of year update: Save worked hard to add 3,000 new Facebook fans to the tally on their Facebook page by the end of the year and they exceeded that number: 3,113 new people became fans. The most successful part of their strategy was tagging people with large social followings in boosted posts to ensure their friends learned about their involvement with Save. This victory would not have happened without that healthy budget for social media promotion.

5,000 new Instagram followers

Instagram is a somewhat new part of the Save digital strategy. The small number of folks who follow @SaveDCsKids – 1,892 to be exact – reflect the fact that this channel has largely been left to the whim of an intern or the spotty focus of a marketing staffer as time allowed. In years past, the log-in information for Instagram hasn't even been properly shared as one intern finishes her summer position and another intern begins his role for the academic year. No cohesive multi-channel strategy had been created and implemented.

This year, Save vows to highlight Instagram as a core part of their online strategy and expects to see significant growth in this channel.

End of year update: taking a quick look at Save's Instagram feed and the number of followers they had on December 31 is all that's needed to see that their goal was too aggressive for follower growth. They did almost double their number of followers from January to December, ending the year with 3,451 followers on this channel, but they fell short of the 5,000 person goal.

New Donors

Save's goal of 1,000 new online donors is part of several grant deliverables and an integral part of the organization's overall growth strategy. The organization usually sees 500-600 new donors a year, so moving that number to 1,000 is ambitious. The Save development team will focus on lower dollar first-time donors to reach this goal as well as a "Refer a Friend" program.

End of year update: Salesforce is the place where the new donor data is kept at Save and it tells a mixed story of fundraising for the past 12 months. Although Save did not reach 1,000 new online donors they had hoped to reach, they did raise more donors online in 2017 than they ever had before (the average online donation to Save this year was almost $50!). If this metric had been focused on a total number of dollars from new donors as opposed to total number of new donors, Save's development team would have blown this one out of the water.

Super Volunteers

Like many great ideas, Save's super volunteer program, Save Stars, was born from a mistake.

During the first few years of Tricia's leadership of Save DC's Kids, she found many DC area activists and advocates who wanted to give time but couldn't afford to make financial donations to the program. Tricia was good at coming up with direct volunteer tasks for each person, helping to prepare school lunches or provide aftercare or even allowing folks with an educational background to serve as teacher training when appropriate.

What Tricia did not do was ever ask these volunteers to help recruit other volunteers. So little by little, the volunteer program dwindled in number. Save couldn't depend on volunteer help because the number of available folks varied so much. The organization didn't have the staff time to actively recruit volunteers at all, let alone those with specific skill sets... so Save Stars was born.

There is an entire grassroots organizing model operating within Save DC's Kids. Existing volunteers who recruit three or more additional volunteers with skills in specific areas during their volunteer engagement with the organization become Save Stars. There is a volunteer-run volunteer onboard process and even a certification ceremony for folks once they move from regular Save volunteer to Save Star status.

Right now, the program includes 71 current volunteers. To grow this program to 100 Save Stars, the existing volunteers will need the skills to leverage their networks and bring new folks into the program.

End of year update: this goal was met in June of this year and by the end of the year, the Save Stars program was so big (129 folks strong), that the Volunteer Engagement Coordinator was able to hire a second staff person to support her work. The grassroots organizing strategy proved to be just what Save Stars needed to shine.

SIMPLY MEASURE

GOAL #1	GOAL #2

GOAL #3	GOAL #4

Q1

Q2

Q3

Q4

REFERENCES

Course Hero. (2014). The best way to measure marketing effectiveness is When it comes to measuring. Retrieved from https://www.coursehero.com/file/p54q9iv/The-best-way-to-measure-marketing-effectiveness-is-When-it-comes-to-measuring/

Docurated. (2015, May 20). Marketing Effectiveness: 30 Experts Reveal Their Top Ways to Measure the Effectiveness of Marketing Campaigns. Retrieved from http://www.docurated.com/whats-your-1-way-to-measure-marketing-effectiveness/

Kelly, M. (2016, November 15). 20 Key Performance Indicators Nonprofit Management Needs to Track. Retrieved from https://www.salsalabs.com/blog/key-performance-indicators-nonprofit-management-needs-to-track

Splitpixel Creative. (2016, September 13). The seven best tools for measuring the success of your digital marketing plan. Retrieved from http://www.splitpixel.co.uk/blog/seven-best-tools-measuring-success-digital-plan/

Sexton, C. (2017, July 19). Phone interview

CONCLUSION

If you want to succeed, you need to be able to see the bigger picture. Smart digital marketing includes a strategy, as opposed to only focusing on tactics and techniques. Just like the whole is greater than the sum of its parts, a solid strategy is more effective than reliance on tactics alone. A good strategy helps you narrow in on your larger goals and checks that your ambitions are aligned. It also includes enough flexibility, so that you can make adjustments along the way in response to changing circumstances.

An organization that wants to make real gains needs a digital strategy that encompasses and responds to the business goals of the organization. In a constantly changing digital landscape, a sharp learning curve is required, as well as an openness to using new tools and techniques. As a practical workbook, *Post With Purpose* is intended to provide a cutting-edge toolbox to match your organization's communications needs.

The lessons in this book are intended to enhance your thinking when it comes to planning and executing a digital strategy for your organization. As the great inventor Benjamin Franklin once said, "If you fail to plan, you are planning to fail!" By charting a step-by-step course tailored to your organization's unique challenges, you will be able to approach challenges armed with knowledge and execute your goals more effectively for the long run.

www.ingramcontent.com/pod-product-compliance
Lightning Source LLC
Chambersburg PA
CBHW031959170526
45157CB00002B/465